CHRISTINE KALAFUS

FLOOD

A MEMOIR

FLOOD

A MEMOIR

CHRISTINE KALAFUS

Woodhall Press | Norwalk, CT

woodhall press

Woodhall Press, Norwalk, CT 06855
WoodhallPress.com
Copyright © 2025 Christine Kalafus

Cover design: LJ Mucci
Layout artist: LJ Mucci

Library of Congress Cataloging-in-Publication Data available

ISBN 978-1-960456-31-1 (paper: alk paper)
ISBN 978-1-960456-32-8 (electronic)

First Edition
Distributed by Independent Publishers Group
(800) 888-4741

Printed in the United States of America

For my mother.

And for all warriors whose armor is a fuzzy sweater.

I am my own microclimate.
Forecast: too warm, probably humid,
ever-present chance of flood.

From *Wake, Siren: Ovid Resung*
by Nina MacLaughlin

Torrington

Naugatuck River

zZZz

SLEEPING
GIANT
MOUNTAIN

Beacon Falls

Seymour

Derby

Ansonia

The Witch House

Housatonic River

Hamden

New Haven

Long Island Sound

1

PROLOGUE

One late summer afternoon a few days before I plunged into my sophomore year at a new college in yet another new town, my father taught me how to change a tire. Afterward, he rummaged around in his tool cabinet and produced my dead grandfather's powerized Louisville Slugger, handing it to me like it was a pair of scissors, or a knife.

"Slide it under the driver's seat," he said, placing the smallest of his trucker caps, part of a collection that hung on a series of nails over his workbench, on my head.

"If you get a flat, put this on. Tuck your hair up underneath it," he said, eyeing my long hair, unruly in the humidity. "You'll be safer wearing the cap—if you look like a man." The baseball bat was self-explanatory.

My armaments didn't end there. One brisk October morning, I woke before dawn. Just an hour earlier, my father had arrived home from his job hauling a tractor trailer full of frozen hamburgers to McDonalds. While he snored in the bedroom he shared with my mother, I palmed his gift in the kitchen: a canister of pepper spray. The instructions on the counter beside it were written in his customary hand—all capital letters.

At ten o'clock at night, after Building Construction 101, I'd walk to my car, avoiding trees and dumpsters and especially large trucks, anything that might conceal a rapist. Between two knuckles of my left hand was my car key, a makeshift knife. In my right hand was the pepper spray, index finger on its white button, ready to advance attack. Safe in my car, I drove away from campus, north on interstate 95, slipping along the silent New Haven harbor, gripping the wheel of my Plymouth Horizon. I had a bat, a cap, and a likely illegally obtained substance to protect me from good Samaritans.

When I wasn't in school or working part-time at an art supply store in the mall, I watched talk shows as if my life depended on them. My favorite shows featured ex-cops. These retired officers dispensed advice on self-defense aimed at professional women living alone—not a nineteen-year-old ballet school dropout and commuting student at a university she couldn't afford, living at home with overprotective parents.

Still, if a perp broke into the house the one and only time I showered with no one else home, how would I defend myself? The only hope for survival, one muscled talk show cop said, was to react instantly, using the razor I shaved my legs with to slice open a serial killer's face. My razor was a petal-pink Daisy with a moisturizing strip. I developed a backup plan: scream and stand menacingly, arms extended, mesmerizing my attacker by brandishing the unusable razor and a bar of extra-gentle Camay.

I never had to use any of it. The powerized bat or the trucker cap. The pepper spray, the razor, or soap. When I was invaded from the inside, I had no protection at all.

ONE

I am bent over, my head in the washing machine, when I feel the pins. I stand quickly, placing my left hand to the odd sensation in my right breast. Fingertips prod. I know what I am touching—the prophecy. It did not come from God; it came from me. When I was ten years old I regaled the kids at recess, repeating what I'd recently overheard at my paternal grandmother's funeral. *Everyone has cancer cells sleeping inside them. It's just a matter of time before they wake up. I probably have more than any of you.* I was popular for a week.

A year before she died, my father brought me to visit Grandma Rose in the hospital in Derby. Derby is one of a handful of mill and manufacturing cities in the geographic area of Connecticut officially known as the Lower Naugatuck River Valley. But everyone who lives there just says The Valley. It's where my father was born and grew up. It's where my mother moved with her parents when she was fourteen so her father could open his own bakery. It's where I was born and lived until I was thirteen.

Once industrious producers of silver, rubber, and heavy machinery, Valley cities and towns dot two rivers—the Housatonic and the

Naugatuck. They rush south, closer and closer to each other before merging in Derby. Derby once pumped out corsets and hoopskirts and welcomed Amelia Earhart at the opera house. Houdini made an appearance.

Derby has the Valley's only hospital. From the sky, Griffin Hospital sits on a hill above the confluence of the Housatonic River and the Naugatuck River, a freckle in the V of a watery stethoscope.

I was born at Griffin and so was my father. His mother, my Grandma Rose, was born in Olcsva, a small rural village in Hungary. In the hospital, my father sat in a chair beside Grandma Rose, but I stood at the foot of her hospital bed, clutching the construction paper get-well card I'd made. With her eyes closed, she waved me closer. Leaning in to kiss her pale cheek, her lash-less eyelids fluttered open and bore into mine. Chemotherapy had turned the whites of her eyes yellow.

Grandma Rose spent her last months at home, dying slowly. She lay in her bed, all the shades drawn, propped up on pillows and wearing a satin bed jacket. I never left empty-handed. All I had to do was touch something and she gave it to me. Nearer the end, all I had to do was glance at something and it was mine. My collection included an Art Deco crystal vanity set replete with weighty faceted perfume decanters that sat on a footed oval mirror, a patchworked stuffed Scottie, and an eighteen-inch-tall blue plastic Siamese cat, its body full of rose-scented bubble bath.

Twenty-one years later in my basement, I don't want chemotherapy, yellow eyes, or to give away all of my possessions. I don't want my three children to watch me die. Trevor is four. The twins haven't arrived yet. I am seven months pregnant.

On the cobwebbed windowsill over the dryer is a hammer. My husband Greg's tools are everywhere. He works in increments, at night and on weekends, turning our dark unfinished basement into a bright clean playroom. Helpless to admire the changes we are trying so hard to welcome, all I can do is stand there. Unable to predict the future, I attempt and fail to relieve the pressure of my enormous belly by pressing into it with my right hand, holding my breast with the other, the wet towels I dropped soaking my slippers.

TWO

My obstetrician insists the pinpricking lump in my breast is a clogged milk duct.

"Don't worry," Dr. Robb says, removing his latex gloves. "I'm sure it's nothing."

"It doesn't feel like nothing," I say from the obstetric table, belly in the air.

"It's nothing," he says, winking, throwing his gloves in the trash. He leans against the countertop, crosses his arms, and smiles. "We'll keep an eye on it. But, really, it's just a clogged milk duct."

It's true that although I still have two months to go, I am already lactating.

"OK," I say, hauling myself up.

So there's a lump, big deal, I say to myself in the car. *He's the one wearing a white coat with diplomas on the wall.* I was raised to not only accept authority, but revere it.

A month later, the lump noticeably larger, Dr. Robb waves my worries away with another purple latex glove. Just after Christmas, Trevor is snuggling with me on a lazy Sunday morning. I tickle him and one of his four-year-old elbows connects with the lump in my right breast. My mouth falls open and my eyes clamp shut. Behind my squeezed eyelids are shooting stars.

A week later, January second, I'm back with Dr. Robb for another heartbeat checkup. My belly is like Mount Everest. Dr. Robb traverses it with a white paper measuring tape, stretching it with the help of a nurse I haven't met before. Together, they laid the tape over my hills and valleys, sternum to pubic bone.

"That lump," I say, bringing my chin to my chest, searching for eye contact with Dr. Robb. "It really hurts."

"Lump?" Dr. Robb says, turning away, clicking a pen, he writes something on a paper attached to a clipboard.

Weren't we supposed to be watching it?

"Here," I say, touching the lump. I'm ten again, standing in front of Grandma Rose's open casket, nine-year old cousin Alison beside me. *I dare you to touch her finger* she says in my ear.

"I'm sure it's nothing," he says, waving his arm, placing the measuring tape into the nurse's open hand like he's a magician and she's his assistant. Struggling to sit up, the nurse takes me by the shoulders and together we bring my body upright. I lock eyes with her.

"Now. I want it checked out *now*."

At the reception desk, she's waiting behind the glass partition. Sliding it open, she hands me a sticky note. "It's just across the street. They've squeezed you in."

I shuffle out of the office and down the hall of this converted 1800s elementary school. I bypass the broad staircase for the elevator. Jaywalk waddling across the New Haven street, I enter a glass and steel building. Inside, all the lights are on motion detectors. The expansive lobby rains darkness. A single light over my head switches on when the elevator opens.

Minutes later I am prone again, my body a mirror for the Ansel Adams poster of Yosemite on the ceiling. The polar opposite of my obstetrician, this doctor is wiry and wears the neon running sneakers I've seen on the feet of college students. He swabs my exposed peasant-sized lactating breast with a numbing agent. At the pinnacle of the lump he inserts a long thin needle.

I've taken the day off from work where I shuffle papers at an insurance office, and proceed through the afternoon shuffling through my house, my belly shapeshifting from mountain to pendulum.

After dinner, Greg and I sit across from one another at the dining room table—our only table—since the kitchen is galley-shaped. There is an ocean of newly washed baby clothes between us. We fold. Trevor runs in from the sunroom asking for a drink. The phone rings and I answer it as I open the fridge, pouring apple juice into a drip-free cup.

Dr. Robb doesn't wait for me to say hello.

"You have to come in tomorrow. The babies have to come out. Pre-operative blood work tomorrow and delivery the next day. The tumor is aggressive. We don't know where else the cancer is."

I can't seem to screw the top on the cup. I abandon it on the counter and hang up the phone. Greg is mid-fold of a tiny onesie. His huge hands place it on the pile. The twins aren't due for another three weeks. They aren't ready. I'm not ready. I don't have time for blood work, twin delivery, or cancer. Greg looks at me. I don't have time for conversation. I have an errand. I whisper, "It's positive," while putting on my coat. As if whispering will make cancer small. I'd only told him about the lump that morning. I have my reasons. Greg doesn't stop me from going out. It's eight-thirty. The store closes at nine.

Mid-afternoon, when I picked Trevor up from daycare, Miss Nancy, the Mother Goose of Sunny Side Up, pulled me aside.

9

"Trevor can't play outside in the snow with the other children because you haven't brought in boots."

Boots. Everything else can wait.

I drive through lightly falling snow to Kohl's. No emotion. Just boots. Inside the store's wet aisle, I spot my treasure. Right hand grabs the last pair of size five navy blue Totes with easy-on handles. My left hand supports my back. The boots are fifty percent off.

At home, Trevor is asleep, a tuft of his brown hair visible above the blankets. Downstairs, I walk past Greg sitting on the love seat staring into space, retrieve the phone from the kitchen, and curl myself into a corner of the larger sofa. Last summer, I nearly drove my car straight into a road race. There had been no security at the intersection, just hundreds of runners.

I'm in a race I didn't sign up for. The only way I can finish is if it's a relay.

I punch buttons on the cordless phone. I speak to my mother. I speak to my cousin Alison. I try to call up the face of the doctor with the needle but the only thing that connects are neon sneakers.

The next morning, Greg and I drop Trevor off to Miss Nancy happily wearing his new boots and head to the hospital. While Greg parks the car, I follow small blue signs down broad corridors to the lab. At the center of an intersection is a raised security guard station. A female guard sits at the center like a queen in a swivel chair. She looks me up and down and throws her head back, releasing a full-throated laugh. I stop walking. Hoisting herself to stand, the guard steps down from her octagonal throne. She purses her lips and produces a slow whistle while resting her hands on ample hips, nodding her head. Her crown of braids dance.

"Whoa, honey. That's what I know for sure. That's a twin belly coming at me."

I don't want to go to the lab. I want to crawl into the lap of this oracle in blue and ask her if I'm going to live. I squeak out, "Lab?"

"Right there, baby," she says, pointing at the door next to me that has *lab* in giant red letters.

Inside, the phlebotomist shakes her head as she assesses my pale, freckled arm.

"What this is, is the Milky Way." Her eyes are violet. "Darlin,' you have baby veins. Pump your fist and I'll get a butterfly." While she chooses a needle with plastic wings from her collection, I pump my fist as directed, wishing I could use it on my obstetrician.

That night, after my parents pick up Trevor, Greg and I go to bed. It's seven PM, but I'm exhausted. Together, we have whisked the house clean of dust, the cobwebs that seem to plague our old house, and errant Legos. The small bedroom next to our holds a pair of white cribs, their mattresses encased in sheets sprinkled with a pattern of blue and yellow dots. Blue and white striped crib skirts conceal a drawer at the bottom of each crib where I stacked shallow rows of premature sized diapers. My small suitcase is packed with several days of clothes and leans against our open bedroom door. Waiting.

Greg reaches over, finds my hand on top of my belly and gathers it up in his. I recall the security guard, her laugh, her knowing. I don't seem to know anything. I hold my belly all night. I don't touch either breast.

Four-thirty in the morning, Greg and I depart for the hospital. Rolling down our street, I wonder about the next time I'll see our house. I once had control. I was once the driver of my life. Now I'm a passenger, an unwilling particle in a sweeping current.

My ass has escaped the johnnie coat and flattens on the edge of the metal operating table. An enormous stainless-steel pendant illuminates my back. Behind me, the anesthesiologist inserts a needle full of medication to numb me from the waist down. Scanning the room to distract myself from the needle moving in my spine, I focus on a hierarchy of scalpels. My emotions are inaccessible, floating in fog. Only actions are clear. I appreciate the scalpels' order, lined up from smallest to largest.

Nurses and doctors with plastic shields covering their faces, like playacting welders, move toward me. Somehow, I am flat on the table. My arms, held in place with straps, are away from my body as if they reach for opposite walls. A nurse sits behind my head, rubbing it. Even though I only know that her eyes are blue and her hands are cool I say, "I'm in love with you. Let's run away together."

Jokes are my comfort zone. She smiles. Anything else I try to say slips from my brain and under the surgery door. Me, Greg, and the nurse are the only people in the room who can't see what's happening backstage—behind the little curtain erected below my chin.

Thirty minutes earlier, my now immobile right hand had signed a paper.

"You don't want to get pregnant on chemotherapy, so sign this," Dr. Robb said. There was a man beside him I'd never met. He could have been a doctor. He could have been the president of the hospital. He could have been the mayor of Nova Scotia.

"I'm having chemotherapy?" My eyes ricocheted between the two men, trying to make contact. Instead, Dr. Robb handed me a piece of paper and a pen. The nameless man nodded his head. I ignored him and addressed Dr. Robb. "I don't want to have my tubes tied. Greg will have a vasectomy, once—" The rest dissolved because Dr. Robb cut me off.

"We'll be in there anyway. And isn't your family complete? You know, after a vasectomy, those little swimmers are still good for a few weeks or more. You could get pregnant."

"Isn't this a Catholic hospital?" I wasn't Catholic. I was stalling.

"Yes, well—" Dr. Robb glanced at the nameless man. "We'll say it was medically necessary. For a damaged uterus."

I'm damaged.

I signed the paper.

From my vantage point on the operating table, I focus on the stainless-steel light. It looks expensive like it belongs in Restoration Hardware. Someone behind the curtain says, "You'll feel some pressure."

It's not pressure. It's turbulence. I go down. I come up. There is a sound of suction. A baby is held above the curtain. Spencer. I hope to one day tell him that he is named after the Golden Age film star Spencer Tracy, which isn't true. Another baby is lifted above the curtain. Parker. I hope to tell him one day that he is named after my first TV crush, Parker Stevenson, which is one hundred percent true.

Someone runs a vacuum in my stomach. The nurses spin from one side of the room to the other, the hems of their operating room smocks flying out like tutus.

"My babies. I can't see my babies," I say, but my throat is dry, my voice thin. The head rubbing nurse has run away without me. "Where is she?" I say. Greg's face hovers over mine. "They're fine." He's crying.

"What's happening?" I say, meaning *what's happening to me.*

"They're peeing on the nurses," Greg says. Operating room laughter.

13

"You're doing just great, Chris." A man's voice. "We're going to tie your tubes now and then we'll remove the tumor."

Asshole. No one calls me Chris except my family.

"I'm leaving," I say. But my arms are stuck. My legs won't do as they're told.

"Christ, that hurts." Someone is playing baseball with my fallopian tubes. I squirm. That gets me two face-masked doctors in view.

"She's getting agitated. Get her under."

This anesthesia tastes like freezer-burned Breyers vanilla bean ice cream.

Blackness.

A spotlight. I am dancing in my ballet recital on the Seymour Middle School stage. But I'm not twelve wearing a cerulean blue lace tutu and sequined tiara with my Valley Dance and Gymnastic School friends, I'm twenty-four and wearing my wedding dress—dancing a solo. Instead of being backlit, there's a fire onstage. It follows me, hotter and hotter, while I perform one arabesque after another. The audience sits with their arms folded in front of their chests. I mutter *tough crowd.*

Now I am in the audience. Sitting on a ripped velvet seat. I trace the pulse of the woman onstage with my eyes. She's not in a wedding dress, but naked on an operating table. I watch her interior combustion. Breath enters her body and travels to her lungs, but instead of exhaling, she holds it. *Don't do that.* My head falls back. My lips open and I exhale an end for both of us.

Or a beginning.

THREE

I should tell you about the house. The first time I saw the house, we were together. Greg drove us to Hamden, a large suburban town outside New Haven. Trevor was five months old and tucked into his car seat, asleep after the day's excitement at the Durham Fair. I was in the passenger seat clutching a stack of grainy black and white house listings and a map.

Our apartment in West Haven was spacious enough for Greg and me, but somehow a single baby made it cramped. After looking at other New Haven area towns, we settled on Hamden. It was close to everything and everybody who mattered most to us. My parents in North Haven, our friends and jobs, but mostly I was drawn to the wildness of the landscape—especially in Mount Carmel, a neighborhood in the northeast part of town.

Mount Carmel was named as a reference to the mount Carmel in the Bible:

So Ahab sent unto all the children of Israel,
and gathered the prophets together on mount Carmel
I Kings 18:20

The mountain range described is in northern Israel. In Arabic it translates to Mount Mar Elias and is home to a UNESCO biosphere reserve. The Mount Carmel in Hamden, Connecticut is home to Sleeping Giant Mountain. Climbing it was one of our first outings as a family of three. Just a few months before house-hunting, we took the path that leads to the belly of the Giant, what the Quinnipiac Tribe call Hobbomock, a stone giant put to rest by a manitou, or good spirit.

According to one legend, Hobbomock had to be put to sleep because he slammed his foot down in anger at the mistreatment of his people by white settlers. In another, his anger was due to white settlers destroying his people's land. The truth is somewhere in the body of the mountain. Either way, the collective legend is that before the manitou put him to sleep, it was Hobbomock's anger induced foot that diverted the Connecticut River at Middletown where it swings wide to the west.

It was June. Greg carried Trevor on his back in a baby harness as we climbed up the Giant's left hip to his belly. At the summit, we ascended the open-air Romanesque viewing tower, what locals call The Castle. Instead of looking out the window-holes as we ascended, I watched Trevor's gently kicking feet, saving the surprise of the view. At the top, Greg turned toward the parapet and a view of the western mountains. I turned toward the wall of arched open-air windows. Splaying my fingers on a stone sill, leaning into the openness, was the wind in the clouds, the skyline of New Haven, and in the far distance a tidal estuary of the Atlantic Ocean—Long Island Sound—a slim line of navy blue.

Four months later on the way to the house listing, we passed the entrance to the Giant.

"Turn here," I said at Dickerman Street. "It's number one-twenty."

Greg pulled the car off Whitney Avenue and up a steep hill with sharp curves. I pulled my nose to the house specs.

Built: 1928. Bedrooms: three. Bathrooms: one. Fireplaces: one.

Fireplace. None of the other houses in our price range had a fireplace. Most of them had massive quantities of asbestos in the basement. Greg stopped the car and put it in park. I dropped the listing.

I unbelted and leaned toward the driver's side window, almost in Greg's lap.

The house sat on a rise of long uncut grass. White and taller than it was wide, even taller trees were visible past its steeply pitched roof. My eyes took in the staircase to the front door, the two stories, four roof lines, and steeply pointed center gable—an architectural detail that I would learn caused the neighborhood kids to call it The Witch House. My eyes travelled to the white painted brick chimney that disappeared into a small side room full of windows. I took in the house's cracked green shutters. I took in its emptiness. The house had Post-medieval English, Gothic Revival, Colonial Revival, Dutch Colonial, and Tudor features. It was wacky.

I didn't even have to see inside. I knew it was meant to be ours.

At the end of a roll of photos I captured of Trevor touching farm animals at the fair, is a single photo that Greg took. In it, I stand on the landing by the front door holding Trevor, my arms overflowing with his plumpness as we face Greg on the front lawn. You can't see it in the photo, but a cord is tied to the front door. It connects to my smile, Trevor's toothless one, and Greg's behind my 35mm Minolta.

Before the closing, we called our auto agent for homeowner's insurance. The agent, in Texas, said to Greg, "You're in a flood zone."

"You need a topographical map," Greg told her. "We're almost two hundred feet above the tiny Mill River. If the Mill floods and reaches us—well the whole town would be under water."

Greg laughed. The agent laughed. I laughed. We got the low-price rate.

FOUR

My awareness of the house as a living thing began the day after we moved in.

That day, and every day, began with my bare feet stepping into the bathroom and onto white and royal blue basketweave tile, each one individually placed into cement. I would sit on the toilet and see patterns emerge. The tile laying wasn't done all in one day. See, over here—the tiles are a little closer together. I have scrubbed these tiles on my hands and knees while imagining two men, side by side, in 1928. Prohibition is waning. They hand each other porcelain tiles and joke about a moonshine break while they finger tile and smoke.

Soaking in the deep porcelain tub, hot bubbles up to my neck, I've imagined the draftsman. He's young and Italian with something to prove because there are two arches in the bathroom. One graces the tub. Another, the toilet. *Perfetto* he says to himself at his ancient Rome inspired drawing. It becomes his signature, like Frank Lloyd Wright and Prairie style.

The sink had no legs. Somehow, it was fastened to the wall. There were two taps and two faucets. The tarnished brass chain remained, but the stopper was long gone. I used a small Tupperware lid to swirl cold and hot water together for do-it-myself drugstore facials.

Standing on the lawn, I've appraised its windows. Each of the twenty-eight mortise and tenon frames was made by hand. The mortise hole and tenon tongue disregard nails and screws, fitting like a tongue in a mouth. Raising a sash, a counterweight lifts, the pulley creaking inside the window casing. Traces of the original green paint show themselves. The green is not forest green, not blue green, but Crayola Jungle Green. The greenest green.

Each window has a pair of extra frames. The screened frames we used in summer and the solid glass frames used in winter. All were labeled with roman numerals in pencil. Corresponding markings were on the house, etched into the exterior trim like hours on a clock.

In addition to the bathroom, there were three upstairs bed-rooms. The staircase met the hall in the middle. Walk down eight creaky steps and you arrive on a small landing. An eighteen-inch square window at child's height looks over the backyard. Take a ninety-degree turn on the balls of your feet and down eight more steps, you land in the living room. Large cast iron radiators ping under each window. The brick fireplace is trimmed in oak.

I would walk through the dark living room, pass the front door, through the dining room, and into the galley kitchen, the sun on my face while I filled the kettle. By breakfast, the sun was at my back, unbroken through the single six-over-one window, while I ate a slice of toast.

After our work, daycare, and dinner was done, Greg, Trevor, and I moved like magnets through to the sunroom's French door. Its doorknob, like all the others, is faceted glass. Touch it, and you cast a spell. Lilacs pushed against the sunroom screens each May, filling the room with flower-shaped shadows and sweet perfume. The fragrance permeated winter moods, even in corners, where things sometimes got stuck. Facing full west, the last of the day's sun passed between pines as if the house's blueprint had been daylight. Safety surrounded us—a mirage.

One and a half miles away, the Sleeping Giant moved a finger. In response, the water table under our house rose, cracking the foundation, undetected.

It was New Year's Eve. I had just put Trevor, now three years old, to bed. I was curled up on the sofa, hands around a book and feet where I liked them, tucked between two pillows. I loved that sofa. Greg and I picked it out before we married. Covered in blue and white checked cotton, it was trimmed in pine with curved legs and giant overstuffed cushions.

Greg came in and sat down. Not on the cushion next to mine, but the far cushion. Leaning forward, elbows on his knees, he clasped and unclasped his hands, staring into the unlit fireplace.

Here.

Here is where I want to freeze us into a still life. Trace the innocence on my face the way I would trace the outline of a bottle in high school drawing classes. I was so sure, so positive of what we were together. Even now, if I went to the drawer and pulled out a pencil and a sheet of paper, I could draw the scene. The muscles in Greg's jaw. The curve of his left bicep through his shirt. His wedding ring. But if I turn an artist's eye on myself, I see no physical details of a woman. In this portrait of our marriage, I see only a girl. But I can't stop the forward motion of time.

"What is it?" I said, not able to register the warning. A prickling of the skin akin to the first desire to scratch a patch of poison ivy. Instead, I registered his mood. It wasn't like Greg to be sullen. Irritable and overworked—yes. Brooding wasn't his style. He turned his head and looked me square in the eye.

"I don't think I love you anymore," he said, adding "There's someone else."

Holy shit. He's gay.

"Holy shit. You're gay," I said, untucking my feet and rooting them to the floor.

"I'm not gay."

"Someone—who is it?" I said.

One beat. Two beats. Three.

"She works with me."

For a second I couldn't connect the hospital with our sofa. The woman worked at the hospital. The same hospital that, as a college freshman, he began work as a security guard in the emergency room. The same hospital where he now had a position that came with an office. I'd maxed out my credit card to buy him the suit he needed for the job interview. The same hospital where Trevor was born. Where Greg had close friends who knew random things about him. Like the young woman he dated before meeting me when we were nineteen. Like how he'd once been Employee of the Month at his high school job at Burger King. They must have known that he didn't love me. Obviously, the woman knew. I was the last to know. I began to shake.

"What's her name?"

He told me and I immediately forgot it.

If I could stop the story in this place of forgetfulness, then I would have to admit I'd been a fool. I'd given up the pleasures of drawing, painting—meeting other creative people. Was I sure I loved the checked sofa? Really, I was floral. It was Greg's idea that a couple was a pair of stripes running in the same direction.

If I could have gone back in time, I would have told that twenty-four-year-old, all fresh college degree and sparkling engagement ring, that lusting after a man didn't mean you had to marry him. It would have been more than enough to admire his healthy ego, self-confidence, and strong body as the first man she had sex with. The one she said goodbye to on the way to other people.

It was only later that I dissected the spark of anger in the center of my chest that came with his confession. That in my family, a woman's denial of herself equaled survival. But in that moment, I only saw a flash of light. I stood up.

"Well, I guess you should go pack a bag and take it over to what's her name's house." I raised my right eyebrow. "I assume you're moving in with her."

"It's over," he said. "I stopped seeing her."

I took two steps to stand in front of him, the back of my knees hitting the coffee table. I could see why he would want to go. Why hadn't I thought of an affair myself? Leave the old house that needed constant repair, leave the responsibilities of daily, relentless parenting. What's her name is new and I was old. That I was thirty didn't seem irrational at all.

I clamped my eyes shut. "Why are you telling me if it's over?"

"I couldn't live with myself. Knowing I'm that guy. A guy who cheats on his wife."

My eyes flew open. I was his confessor. The robe of Greg's Roman Catholic childhood—his altar boy self—had appeared. His head was down, almost reaching his knees. There's no sin in breaking a sacred vow if you don't intend reconciliation. His confession wasn't about me at all. It was about a boy who wanted forgiveness. But it was also about a man who wanted out.

"How many times," I said, staring at the wall.

"How many times did you fuck her?"

Silence.

"Three times."

The feeling of poison ivy crawling up my arm was replaced with a new sensation. The desire to illicit a stab. I wanted to injure him so he would feel the immediacy of my own, raw wound. I had been taught that marriage was sharing everything.

"Get out." My voice was low, but hysteria pulsed at the back of my throat. Greg looked at me in surprise. Hell, I was raised Protestant. He couldn't compete.

"You know what?" I said, moving away from him, pacing the room. "Actually, this will work. It'll be great. Better than great." The smile that stretched across my face could have been nothing but crazed.

"You know how my parents have been talking about buying a three-family house as an income property. Trevor and I will live on the first floor and I'll oversee the tenants. Everybody wins!"

I didn't know where my confidence was coming from. I didn't want to leave my house. And I definitely didn't want to oversee tenants. If Greg's confession was a shock, it was another to discover how easily I imagined a life without him in it.

"Are you leaving, or what?" When he didn't move, I did. Striding from the living room I made for the kitchen and the basement stairs. At the washer and dryer, I yanked clothes from the laundry basket and threw them into the washer. My marriage was falling apart, but I needed clean underwear.

Greg appeared in the basement. He moved silently from the corner where we kept the luggage. He held a small duffel. *Drakkar Noir* written on the side. The bag came with a boxed set of cologne I'd bought him one birthday.

When had he packed the duffel—when I was making dinner? Reading Trevor *Where the Wild Things Are* for the thousandth time?

The ending of our marriage was like the end of an Agatha Christie mystery. The murderer has exposed himself. But unlike Miss Marple, I haven't solved the mystery of our dead marriage in time. By studying social control in college, Greg knew me well enough to predict the outcome. I didn't know him at all. I studied art.

I didn't have a bag stashed in case of a marriage emergency. Suddenly, I didn't see him as a shameful, penitent child, but a selfish man. If I were in the role of confessor, I would do my job and judge. I rested my eyes on his lips. They looked different. They looked like liars.

"You don't think you love me anymore?" The lower half of my body was a tree trunk. My upper pitched back and forth waving in a hurricane. "Bullshit." I marched upstairs.

I returned to the sofa. Now Christmas made sense. I'd practically had to beg him to take a photo of me holding Trevor at my aunt's house. In the picture, both of us are beaming. When I think of the picture, all I see are shadows. Already, everything had a cast. Before his affair, we bought this stupid sofa. Before he had an affair we bought this house. Before he set off a bomb under our life, I cared what he thought. Probably too much.

Since we met at nineteen, I'd given his moods and desires center stage. I sank into the cushions, wrapped my arms around my knees and wondered what the hell had happened to me. *I Am Woman Hear Me Roar* had been the anthem of my childhood. Then I went to college and a sexy guy showed me his penis. It was probably hereditary.

By kindergarten I discovered the best way to hurt my mother. I'd been sent to my room for something, like wearing good clothes to play outside in, and decided I'd had enough punishment. Huffing down the basement steps, my mother looked up at me beneath a length of telephone cable my father strung up for her. His blue telephone repairman shirts drip-drying between the rafters.

"I'm not going to college!" I screamed at her.

"Oh, yes you are!" she screamed back, her shoulder-length brown hair coming untucked from behind her ears.

I wanted to be a ballerina princess who married a ballet prince. As a result, my mother came home with *Free to Be . . . You and Me.* The album, by Marlo Thomas, was made for children with songs, skits, and poems that encouraged individuality and the removal of gender biases. But when Carol Channing recited

> *Your mommy hates housework,*
> *Your daddy hates housework,*
> *I hate housework, too.*
> *And when you grow up, so will you.*

I recited along while the prince's dinner of a plastic drumstick cooked in my cardboard kitchen, mopped the floor with my robe, and diapered Baby Alive. Toy companies who delude millions of children into believing that fresh baby shit smells like peaches should be sued for restitution.

Soon after, my mother cut her hair into a shag shorter than Jane Fonda's and enrolled in classes at Naugatuck Valley Community College to earn a degree as a nutritionist. After dinner, she'd sit on the floor in front of the master bedroom bureau with large plastic charts illustrating the nutritional makeup of individual foods she needed to memorize decorating the rag rug.

Cheerios sprinkled with sugar were out. Grape Nuts covered in a wheat germ blanket with Carnation powdered milk were in. Liver for dinner. Dessert was once baked apples masquerading as shrunken heads. Then she became pregnant with my sister and quit college. "I couldn't do it all," she told me.

The shape of my marriage was decided by the challenges I saw her face and those of all the other women I knew: husbands came first. Then children. Whatever was left over was divided like an archaic thermometer I once dropped. Tiny balls of mercury skittered across the floor, impossible to gather. The small *Ms.* icon representing the Ms. Foundation for Women at the bottom of my *Free to Be . . . You and Me* album had a sharp uphill climb.

And yet, my mother's dream of a college education eventually became my dream. If I graduated, I would be the first person, on either side of my family, to do so. My father hoped I'd study something practical, accounting for instance. I memorized the three types of ancient Greek architectural order, sliced up Color-aid pre-painted papers for studying color theory, and learned to draw with my opposite hand. My mother married at twenty. So did her mother. Because I waited to marry until after college, I was four years older. I'd never been shown—up close—an alternative.

And no one divorces. Instead, they celebrate fiftieth wedding anniversaries. They cut their hair in slightly softer versions of their husbands' haircuts and begin wearing brown rubber soled lace-up shoes. The view of myself from the sofa was that of a naïve thirty-year-old woman with two hands overflowing with nothing. Failing at marriage and an insurance job she kept because it was safer than the risk of a creative life. I couldn't have sunk any lower into that sofa.

When I was six, my father made me a two-story dollhouse with leftover brown paneling and plywood. It had no hinged façade, no delicacy. This was no Barbie Dream House. Four rooms up and four rooms down, its blueprint was a + sign. Instead of Barbie, anemic Ken, and their Puff 'n Play inflatable furniture, I went for something older. Swiping wooden spools from my mother's sewing basket, I unwound and discarded the thread. The spools became a kitchen table base, a pair of nightstands, a plant stand.

My great-grandmother gave me a miniature enamel robin's egg blue pot with a turned brass handle. Its matching lid was replete with a tiny brass knob. Nestled beneath the lid were diminutive brass tongs. Anything that could fit in my palm bewitched me. I continued my worship of manageable households well into my teens.

When I was thirteen, my parents relocated our family to northern Virginia. My parents told my sister and me that there was more opportunity being so close to Washington, D.C. But I'd overheard my father say that if they didn't get away from the Valley now, they never would. Like the Valley was an abusive boyfriend. When I was eighteen, the year before everything changed again, and we returned to Connecticut, my mother's childhood friend Diane visited. While my mother was at work, I entertained Diane by driving her to Occoquan. I told her there was a restaurant with the world's best club sandwiches, but really, the draw was Mountain Valley Miniature Shop. I dragged her in there, and she watched me swoon over 1:12 scale electric chandeliers and tester beds with moveable curtains.

My prized possession was a reproduction cherry four-poster bed. After hand-sewing a mattress from a piece of threadbare sheet, I stuffed it with craft store feathers I snipped into wisps. Applying my needle, I produced pillows, pillowcases, and a flat sheet. Each item had double hems and decorative stitches using a fine-gauge needle, its eye barely large enough to allow thread.

My dollhouse was long gone. But that didn't stop me from moving Greg around like a doll. If he came back, he wasn't going to sleep in our bed. I picked him up and moved him from the basement to the unheated room behind the detached garage where I stored broken furniture. If I could have reduced our house and Greg into miniatures, I could have everything the way I wanted it to be.

Greg walked into the living room and sat down on the cushion next to me. I stood up again. The coffee table was between us, but there was something else between us. The fairy tale I had been fed. A wedding is the end because happily ever after doesn't deserve a story. The free to be—driven enough to put herself through college—me. She was my shadow. If there is a ghost in any of the houses I have lived in, it is my shadow—dehydrated and transparent—who moves between worlds in the living room of the Witch House.

I saw my own fortune and felt a strange power, foreign as wisdom in an antique language. I read it. Betrayal was precise: pinpoints of black. No ambivalent gray. I didn't see red as I've heard people do. Greg extended his arms. I walked around the coffee table and into them. That's how easy it was to surrender. The surrender was his.

We remained like that for a while. Greg on the edge of the sofa cushion, his arms around my hips, his head resting on my belly. My arms remained at my side. Then my eyes fell on something unexpected—the softness of the crown of his red-haired head. A softness I rarely saw because he is six-foot-one and I am five-foot-five. It was the softness that threw me. It persuaded me to straddle him and push against his chest until he reclined. I kissed him. Hard. He carried me upstairs.

Often, I cry out with the release of an orgasm. But not this time. Something inside me had split.

FIVE

Shouting has always seemed to me like evidence of derangement. By middle school, I didn't recognize anger as a legitimate emotion. It transformed into sadness and bubbled up, manifesting as tears. Anytime I felt the urge to shout, I compressed it into a small space and carried it around. By the time I was eighteen, a shout became a migraine and resulted in me kneeling in front of a toilet, vomiting, and then taking to my bed for hours. Sometimes, if I was lucky, a shout became bronchitis with a laryngitis chaser. I sank into the pleasure of hearing every other word become air.

In the weeks after Greg's confession, lots of sex, and joint counseling sessions with a therapist, I became a happy-acting, easy-going, whispering mute. Below my calm, anger lay defrosting. We made stilted conversation, we made our paychecks stretch, and I made up my face every morning in a bathroom that resembled a temple. Even if I wanted to yell, I no longer knew how.

Greg grew up in a house of yelling. The middle of five children, all constantly arguing, wrestling, and laughing at each other. Their dogs and father barking. When Greg or one of his siblings elicited the tears of another, the one responsible didn't apologize. They got angry. *I didn't hit you that hard.* The one who inflicted the pain acted preyed upon. As the middle child, he is the steady part of the pyramid—most of the time. His nature is to promote justice, a true Libra. When he felt his father's hand was too heavy, Greg left—beginning when he was thirteen—for days. He'd ride his bike thirty miles round trip to stay with his girlfriend's parents.

The mostly peaceful, optimistic and contemplative house I grew up in meant that bad moods were taken for grenades. If my sister or I had one, it needed to be removed from the premises and detonated. In Virginia, this meant a long drive to the Blue Ridge Mountains followed by an ice cream cone.

Once, in high school, I detonated it myself. I wanted to take Amtrak from D.C. to visit Alison. My mother refused. I marched down the hall to my bedroom and slammed the door—something I'd never done. Spinning toward my bed, my left hand connected with the corner of the bureau. I collapsed on the bed, my roar silent. The next morning, my mother silently took notice of the perfect circle of a bruise on my hand at breakfast. It was a year before I showed it to a friend's father—a doctor—when I was there for dinner.

"You broke this bone," he said, cradling my hand gently, pointing to a small knob northeast of the wrist. "You'd have to re-break the bone." I took my hand back and picked up my fork.

"Doesn't it bother you?" he said.

I shrugged. "Only when it rains."

Greg and I stepped carefully through our house, but doing so didn't stop our household from opening to the elements. I became a person who had nightmares. Nightmares that would wake me up at three o'clock in the morning—the hour of desperation—and take me downstairs, where I would sit on the radiator under the set of windows in the dining room. One foggy night, a shadow emerged from the trees. Before I registered the figure as a drunk college kid, loping up the hill from the bar at the bottom, I pressed my nose to the thick glass of the old window, sure it had been an animal.

SIX

The foundation of our house had two-foot-thick walls. The floor, however, was a thin layer of cracked cement over dirt. When it rained, I'd rush to the basement to check for evidence of water. The cracks were barely noticeable when it was dry. But even a light rain resulted in cracks that oozed. Small puddles formed in shallow dips before travelling in every direction, eventually forming a two-inch deep pond.

When we had been in the house for a year, I was returning from a walk with Trevor when I noticed our elderly neighbor outside. She stood over a small manhole in her driveway. Steering the stroller closer, I noticed that the lid—cross-hatched and heavy—looked to be made of iron.

"Hi, Mrs. Peterson. What's that?" I said, standing on my left leg, stretching my right hamstring by bringing my heel to my butt.

"This is where they used to come. The spring runs from the top of the street and continues down to the Mill River."

"Who used to come?" I said, switching feet.

"Everyone around here. It's just us now."

Mr. Peterson appeared in the doorway of their garage with his walker, an empty plastic jug hanging from one finger. Before I could apply the brake to the stroller, Mrs. Peterson retrieved the jug from her husband and returned to the manhole. Using both hands she lifted the lid and rested it back on its hinge. She knelt on the pavement and lowered the jug into the hole. I could see the rushing water, just a foot down. Bringing the full jug up, she closed the lid and stood. "We didn't charge, but no one comes anymore."

Before I could think to ask more questions, she was gone, and so was Mr. Peterson. A for sale sign appeared in front of their vacant house.

Across the street was Margie. One spring day I was pulling the mail from our mailbox, when she ran up to me. We often saw each other around noon when I sped out of the parking lot of the insurance office a few miles away and came home for lunch. Margie was between shifts. The school bus barely fit in her short driveway.

Margie knew everything about everyone. She confirmed Mrs. Peterson's story about neighborhood people lining up for spring water, confirmed the changing hours of our mail lady, and what the status was of the people on the corner who hadn't paid their property taxes. Margie conducted her knowing in nylon track suits.

"Did you have lunch with the girls in the office yesterday?" she said, smiling.

If I told her the truth—that I went to the bank to deposit my paycheck—she would have applied her various thumbscrew skills and I would have spit out my hourly rate against my will.

"Yes."

"Well, you missed him. The old man who built your house. His daughter brought him by. She drove a Buick LeSabre."

"What? How did you know it was him?"

"I saw him looking at your house. What if he was going to rob it?"

"What else did he say? What was his name? Did he say anything else?"

I'd been insatiably curious about the red and yellow flowered wallpaper in the kitchen that we'd decided was easier to sheetrock over than remove, about the furnace our oil man said had been converted from a coal burner, and about the scent of cigarette smoke that hovered by my side of the bed. I was excited. I shouldn't have been.

"I don't remember his name," Margie opened her arms wide. "But his birthday was last week. He just turned ninety-eight!"

If I had been home, I could have asked him how he'd gotten the piano into the sunroom. As Trevor became a toy-collecting toddler, we needed to use the sunroom as a playroom. Which meant the upright piano we barely acknowledged when we moved in needed to be moved out. But rolling it in either direction would hit a wall or window. I phoned an uncle who was a pianist and made his living by piano repair. He drove over to appraise our cumbersome asset.

"Humidity has ruined it," he said.

The only way to get it out of the sunroom was in pieces. The dismantling began. We removed the veneer layer by layer until the piano was a skeleton. Stuck in its exposed keys and string was a child's spelling test. Written at the top was *Sheila* and the year—1960.

When Greg and I closed on the house, to my disappointment, the sellers didn't come. They'd signed the papers in advance. Digging through our mortgage paperwork, I found the sellers' name and address on Cape Cod. I wrote a letter and tucked the spelling test inside.

I received a letter back.

*Thank you for your letter and Shiela's paper. I'm so happy that
you like the house and are happy living there. We bought the house
from an older woman named Catherine. Her husband built it with another
man, but soon afterward, her husband died, leaving her with two children.
She subsequently took in three foster children. She brough up five children
there without a husband. She did not want to sell, but her children felt she
had to, and the passing of papers was a most sad affair. I remember wanting
to say, "Oh, forget all this—you can just stay on with us!"*

*Anyway, the house had not been touched since it was built in 1928.
It had the original wallpaper, lights and shades, and was very dark and dim.
All the oak woodwork was black from polish and dirt. So, we scrubbed. When
we moved in, we had four children. We had two more, so we brought up six
children there.*

*Since the children grew, I've been on the Cape, and when Patrick retired, he
joined me. The house hasn't had a woman's touch for some time, which may
explain some things about it.*

*The piano was my mother's and all the children took lessons on it. I hope you
can get it working again.*

*Enclosed is a key, only a common one, but it belongs in the sunroom door. It
has always lived in that keyhole.*
*   -Ann*

I tipped the envelope upside down and a heavily tarnished brass
skeleton key landed in my palm. She hadn't answered my questions
about the basement.

A month after Greg admitted his infidelity, I walked into the local bookstore, wondering where they shelved the books that saved lives. I passed shelves with books that had once rescued me from disappointment, frustration, and boredom. But Jane Austen, Candace Bushnell, and Helen Fielding just weren't up to this job. Climbing inside *Pride and Prejudice, Sex and the City,* and *Bridget Jones' Diary,* I joined the heroines in places I'd never been—a gentleman's farm in Hertfordshire, a Manolo Blahnik store, and a love triangle. As strong as Elizabeth Bennett, Carrie Bradshaw, and Bridget Jones were at entertaining, they couldn't teach me to swim. I found serious survival—Self Help—way in the back.

Standing between the stacks, I couldn't find the place to start. I sank to the floor. Where were the real heroines when you needed them? I was angry and scared, but I was mostly heartbroken. A small child ran down the aisle, laughing as he flung off his mittens and hat, dropping them like knitted breadcrumbs. My brain was fuzzy. I wondered about the decision to place books about marital strife next to the children's section.

I raised myself up to my knees. On a shelf labeled Marriage/ Relationships were workbooks with spiral bound spines. Each cover had a version of white hetero couples in soft focus wearing matching sweaters on a beach. Only one book looked no nonsense. I headed for the checkout with *Surviving Your Husband's Affair* tucked under my armpit.

Waiting in line, I thought about her. The woman whose name I couldn't remember. Just the day before I'd barged in on Greg in the bathroom, his face covered in shaving cream and holding a razor, while I shook and demanded to know if she was beautiful. If he loved her. If she was thin. And what the fresh hell her name was. He said she had curly hair. That she was bigger than me. Which could have meant that she was tall, or fat and tall, or fat and short, or that she looked exactly like me but had bigger breasts. He told me her name and I know that I know it. That I can remember if I just try harder, but every time I do, it slips away like an ice floe.

Coming up behind was a couple I recognized from church. I grabbed the latest issue of *National Geographic* and placed it on top of my self-help book. The cover of the magazine featured a baby gorilla. "Orphan Gorillas: Fighting to Survive in the Wild." I was pathetic. My book camouflage was even more pathetic. That baby gorilla was like wearing neon yellow. It was winter, so obviously I wore clothes. But I might as well have been naked carrying that crinkly plastic Barnes & Noble bag to my chest striding to my car.

SEVEN

My mother's wedding dress resides in a long gold metal suitcase with a plastic handle like those on vintage lunch boxes. "Don't you dare open it," she warned me whenever she cleaned out the attic and the box appeared in the hallway by the pull-down staircase.

"It's vacuum sealed. If you open that box, the dress will be ruined."

I imagined the dress breathing inside. If I opened it, all the air would rush out and the dress would die.

She knew my fingers itched to touch it. At five, I had a reputation for touching things I shouldn't have. Shiny red Delicious apples at the IGA. Glass display cases at the Yale Peabody Museum. The Hummel figurines she placed on a three-tiered shelf, tantalizingly over the sofa.

I was trusted until she was cleaning the top of the refrigerator and brought the large blue and white porcelain soup tureen down from its unused position, placing it in the center of the kitchen table like the crown jewels. I was on my feet as soon as her back was turned, the soles of my Grasshopper sneakers slipping on the chair's maple seat, hands unable to resist the attraction of the tureen's curved porcelain spoon decorated with blue hand-painted flowers.

When she turned around, the ladle, exotic as a swan, was in two pieces.

Satisfying my desire for my mother's wedding dress began by disobeying her biggest rule. Her privacy. My parent's bedroom was a sanctuary. The bed always made. No toys allowed. The door almost always closed. But I knew there was something accessible in there—in the bottom drawer of her nightstand. My parents' wedding album.

My sister's birth provided the required distraction, allowing my stealth to rise to the surface. To sneak a look, I couldn't perform the behavior modeled by my mother, grandmothers, or great-grand-mother. I didn't politely ask to see it, sitting on the scratchy tweed sofa turning the pages by addressing the top right corner of the page with the tip of an index finger, lifting its edge, running the backs of my fingers down its underside while flipping another leaf, reverentially sweeping my eyes across the formal images, the album's spine resting between my pressed together thighs.

When my mother was tending to my baby sister, I crept into my parent's bedroom and removed the heavy white album from the drawer, my legs splayed on the braided rug in the W position that osteopaths consider dangerous—it weakens the joints and can cause a lifetime of pain. A pain that never touched me. My fingers lifted off tabletops while my palms remained flat. Backbends were my specialty. These hypermobile tricks were my calling cards. My entre to coveted elementary school birthday parties in homes where the girls had Barbie Townhouses, inground pools, and their own dogs.

With the album on the rug before me, I flipped the pages from the bottom. I stroked the fabric of my mother's wedding dress through the photographs. The album was a window to my mother before she was a mother. I looked for evidence of the mother I knew, my nose close to the pre-ceremony photos where she stood between my grandparents pinning a corsage of pink roses on my maternal grandmother. That girl wasn't my mother. I looked for her in the photo where she smiled, one of my great-grandmothers on either side. Not there. Walking down the aisle with my grandfather, the professional baker who had made her wedding cake. Nope. Not there either. I flipped until I found her.

My mother—a bride with a mischievous glint in her eye—shoving cake into the groom's mouth. His right hand gently touches her tiny waist. He's being delicate, tender, feeding her cake with his fingertips. His eyes are closed. The bride faces him, her left hand is in a slight fist. Her right hand disappears into his mouth. Her right eye, closest to the camera, is closed. Her left eye is open. Her mouth—those apple cheeks—are engaged. She laughs at him with cake in her mouth.

This is the mother I knew at five, six—ten, twelve. My mother acted like a child, especially in her parent's house. The mother who teased me because I wouldn't try tapioca even though I loved the celadon bowl my grandmother made it in. Loved its thick green glass with white edges, glossy Saran wrap curling on top with condensation droplets underneath, hanging like half-moons. My grandmother gave me chocolate ice cream. My mother, sitting next to me, spooned tapioca into her mouth. When no one but me was looking, she opened her mouth, tapioca rolling on her tongue.

In Virginia, she turned up the volume. My father was gone for weeks at a time, hauling empty refrigerator cases, shampoo, or customized wheelchairs to California. In Connecticut, my mother had been a woman of public propriety, even if she was childlike in private. At ten years old, I hadn't been allowed to leave the house without wearing a slip if I wore a skirt—even if it was denim.

Sunday drives in Connecticut as a family of four became Sunday drives with my sister and me. Heather in the back seat with

Bun-Bun, her giant, love-worn stuffed rabbit, and me in the front seat taking control of the radio. We always headed to the Blue Ridge, skirting the edge. "Let's drive until we run out of gas," my mother would say, rolling her window all the way down.

It never failed that she'd take a wrong turn and end up on a dirt road. We flew past shacks with chickens in the front yards and rainwater barrels, getting lost on the lookout for adventure. Somewhere, in the bowels of Quantico, is a surveillance video of fourteen-year-old me in cutoff jeans and a halter top grasping a chain link fence while my sister kicks pebbles in the pale dirt with her sneakers, a cloud of dust surrounding us, our mother in a plaid skirt and blouse, shading her eyes at the sign *keep out, government property.* "How do you think we get inside?" She asked us.

By the middle of my freshman year in high school, I'd made one good friend. Rae-Ann didn't believe me when I said my mother was crazy. I was a little afraid of this new mother, and never invited friends home. Afraid she would break into song, letting loose with a tune her southern grandmother taught her and she tortured me with.

> *I knew a man, six feet tall—*
> *he lay in the parlor with his feet in the hall.*
> *How am I doin', hey hey*
> *A doodly, doodly, do!*

Below the Mason-Dixon Line, my father on the road, my mother had become someone else—a vaudevillian—bent over, slapping her knees, tapping her left foot. Looking you right in the eye as she poked you in the ribs.

I took a chance. My mother seduced Rae-Ann with buttermilk pancakes, real New England maple syrup, and tall glasses of cold whole milk. Once my new friend was in a sugar coma, my mother announced, "Let's go for a ride—wouldn't that be fun?"

No. That would not be fun. But there was no arguing. Rae-Ann sat between my mother and me. Heather retained her sole dominion of the back seat. All the windows rolled down; we took off. Vienna, through Aldie, skirting the Snickersville Turnpike to route 50. Middleburg—quaint, historic, and extra horsey—wasn't far enough. The mountains were my mother's magnet. Entering the Blue Ridge Parkway, she'd stick her head outside her window, speedometer hovering at eighty miles an hour, close her eyes and breathe in the mountains. I clutched my door handle.

"Let's bounce!" she said.

I covered my face with my hands and sank into the vinyl upholstery. Rae-Ann poked me with her elbow and mouthed *bounce?* The horror began. My mother and sister sat straight up in their seats—stone faced—bouncing up and down as if their butts had springs. Rae-Ann laughed. Hard.

"Now, Rae-Ann," my mother said, "The rule is you can't laugh. We're going to pass that car, but don't laugh. Just bounce."

Jesus Christ.

My mother stomped the gas and we cruised slowly past an entire family in a station wagon, while my mother, my sister, and Rae-Ann bounced. I was no longer visible. My seat belt was wrapped around my armpits and my butt was on the floor. With the station wagon and its inhabitants in the rear view, my mother let out a whoop. "Did you see their faces!"

"Why didn't you tell me your mother was so much fun?" Rae-Ann said.

Another of my mother's rules was no makeup. Not for her and definitely not for me. Then she decided to become a Mary Kay Image Consultant. The taboo was lifted. No more stabbing myself in the eye with a mascara wand when my school bus hit a pothole. I wasn't only sanctioned to wear makeup, I was recruited.

Box after box of Mary Kay filled the living room of our ranch house full of tantalizing dusty pink glossy boxes of foundation, toner, and palettes of eyeshadow. Unlike Maybeline or Cover Girl, the Mary Kay eyeshadow didn't come with a plastic applicator with a piece of crappy foam at one end. They came with a magic wand. Three-and-a-half inches long, and tapered on one end, the opposite end had a finely bristled straight edged brush that retracted. The eyeshadow had to be mixed with drops of water with the brush before it could be applied to the eyelids. I was hooked.

Convincing my mother to pay me thirty dollars per UPS delivery was easy. I opened every large box, removed and organized each product, applied her gold embossed label, and stacked them on the pink metal Mary Kay shelving unit hanging on the back of her closet door. To prepare for the UPS man, I doused myself in Babe perfume. She took me with her to complimentary facial parties. I set up personal mirrors for each woman in attendance on hostesses dining room tables all over northern Virginia. Halfway through her sales pitch, my mother would give me the sign and I would demonstrate the *upward sweeping motion*—the Mary Kay way—to slather on face cream.

I imagined driving a pink Cadillac, the sign of a truly successful Image Consultant. My mother and me grew up, becoming adults at the same time.

My parents' wedding album was a window, but it was also a door. Just before my own wedding, I examined the pictures for the first time in more than a decade. There was my mother—Carol Lee—twenty years old. She worked for her father in his bakery wiping down mixers, cleaning walls. There was my father—Alan Charles—twenty-one years old. He worked for Sunbeam and drove a bread truck.

There was that familiar object of fascination—her wedding dress. Simple matte white satin, a scoop neckline with a bolero of scalloped lace. On her head was an open-crown pillbox with fine tulle sprouting underneath.

Six years in—my marriage on a cliff—I didn't need to look at my mother's wedding album. The images left a maternal imprint. Like a sun-print, a cyanotype, the oldest non-silver blueprinting that by alchemic reaction produces a positive and negative. Block the bride from the sun—keep her safe. The sun's too hot and she's sensitive.

The images come anyway. Enter the Wallingford Congregational Church. A wedding is multiple ceremonies at once: flickering candles, cascades of flowers tacked to the ends of each pew—yes, enter the bride. Walk toward the groom. On the groom's side, the Roman Catholics are looking for kneeling benches. Congregationalists don't kneel. We eat real bread and drink real wine. But hell, we all break vows. *I promise to love, to cherish*—what about the Christian virtue of forgiveness? For some reason, we don't say *I promise to forgive.*

I drink the potion to the last drop. Something old, borrowed, blue. A vintage 1920s fake pearl bracelet with two frosted glass dangling hearts that I bought in Georgetown as a teenager. My cousin Amy's crinoline from her wedding, and an ice-blue rose glued to a garter that kept falling down my thigh. The music— *Rhapsody on a Theme of Paganini* from the movie *Somewhere in Time,* a movie Greg loved. So romantic it sticks to your teeth like saccharine. Fitting—my family believes in sugar. And in homemade cake. Mix all the families and pour them in a pan. This is what you get: a twenty-minute ceremony where the Catholics wonder when the priest will appear like Superman from behind the altar to bless the union.

The reception won them over. JD Souther sang *Smoke Gets in Your Eyes* from a cassette as dry ice was let loose across the dance floor. The picture I want—one of the alchemic reaction where two souls become one—I don't get. She becomes him and he retains himself. The picture I have is me in a leaving outfit, pretending to be grown-up. I'm dreamy, damp, and vaguely sexless. Certainly not lusty. Wholesome.

"Mom, in this picture, the one of you walking out of the church with Dad. What were you thinking?"

"That I couldn't wait to get the hell out of there. I couldn't wait to be free."

EIGHT

The cocoon formed methodically, instinctively, like a spider wrapping its prey. Layer by cotton layer, whenever Greg and I spoke to each other without walking away. Whenever we played with Trevor, Greg's shoulder near mine, we entered an illusory space where betrayal didn't exist.

On a warm February day, I'd just returned from a walk on my lunch break and sat down at my desk when Greg phoned. He never called me at work. "I think I'm having a nervous breakdown," he said. I laughed into the receiver. There was a co-worker on each side of me. No one at work knew what I was dealing with at home. "I want to be with you, but—"

"There are no buts about it!" I said like a game show host announcing *you just won—a brand new car!*

My manager smiled. "You two are such lovebirds, it makes me sick."

I batted my lashes at her and gripped the phone with both hands. There was something familiar about this situation. Oh, right. The plot of a movie I would never watch.

"I think I need to go home," Greg said.

I told him to leave Trevor at daycare. "I'll pick him up," I said.

Hours later, with Trevor chowing down on Teddy Grahams and watching Blue's Clues in the sunroom, I sat with Greg at the table—the empty living room a shock absorber between us and our child. I still wore my suit. Crossing my legs, the nude nylons whispered against the back of my knee. Greg wore holey sweatpants and a drab green pullover that was all stretched out at the neck. I couldn't look him in the eye. My eyes bore into the seam of his shirt where the seam joined the collar and shoulder. I crossed my arms in front of my chest. He tucked his hands under his thighs.

My tendency had always been to fill silence. The discomfort that came from attending two elementary schools, two middle schools—first in Connecticut, the second in Virginia—a southern high school, capped off by with a year at Northern Virginia Community College and the rest at University of New Haven, meant I had become adept at managing my discomfort. Usually by making fun of myself.

On the first day of third grade, I sat down at a long cafeteria table in a strange school while everyone stared. Opening my pint of milk, I chugged. Releasing the carton from my mouth, I smacked my lips and said, "Ahh, just like mother used to make."

No one said a word until Kimmie Pisarski—the boss of the third grade—pointed at me and said, "Now that is funny." We became fast friends. And I needed a friend. With a giant gap between my two front teeth, freckles, and a German last name that was pronounced the same as the famous TV dog of our parents' generation and in constant reruns, I assumed I'd been born to be teased. In my last school, I'd heard "Lassie, come home!" been tripped during recess, was pushed off the ends of bus seats into muddy aisles, and called a bitch.

In my dining room, waiting for Greg to speak, I realized I wasn't uncomfortable. My job was no longer to alleviate his discomfort. I'd graduated to stoicism.

Greg opened his mouth, but nothing came out. He closed it and opened it again.

"I wake up every morning knowing that I am a man who cheated—that this is who I am now." He had a vacant look. His body was in the room. The rest of him was in outer space.

There are at least fifty synonyms for *survive*. None of them portray a man and a woman sitting at their Amish-made dining table chosen together and purchased with the proceeds of a yard sale. I believed that because Greg said his affair was over, the stress would be over if we would just let it. Believing something is to accept it. To presume, conclude, deduce, understand, gather, comprehend, attach weight to, count on, fall for, have faith in, take as gospel, take at one's word—take for granted.

We weren't in a cocoon. We were in a darkroom, our future a strip of undeveloped film. All the focus was on him. There was no us. There was no we. I'd never confronted a real crisis before. It was becoming obvious that the fallout doesn't necessarily happen right away, in the liquid heat. It may reveal itself in the icy quiet. Threatening clouds don't always disappear at sunrise.

That evening, once Trevor was asleep, the clouds stopped hovering over the house and came in through the chimney.

"You're such an asshole," I said.

"What the fuck do you want from me?" He said.

"I hate you," I said, shaking my head.

After church in fifth grade, I used to play with a girl named Cherry. Cherry came to church with her grandparents who she visited once a month and loved hymns.

"I hate my teacher," I said to Cherry, balancing on a tree trunk behind the church.

"You can't hate your teacher. You can't even say hate," Cherry whispered, even though we were alone.

"Fine! I hate the devil. I hate hell!" I said, picturing my teacher Mrs. Brown while I pointed a stick at random trees. Cherry accepted this like the good Puritan she was.

Telling Greg I hated him, which wasn't true, meant that like him, I was becoming someone I didn't recognize. But we weren't the only ones who changed.

We received a call from Trevor's pre-school. He'd bitten one of his friends.

We made an appointment for marriage counseling to save our son, if not our marriage. Unable to afford a babysitter, we could barely afford pre-school, I had to come clean with my parents. I'd been avoiding them.

The one time I tried to be secretive, a police officer came to the house and informed my parents that their eighteen-year-old ballet student daughter, who didn't shave her legs above the knee—had been busted for drinking underage in a bar.

"How did you even get in?" My mother said, cold washcloth on her forehead, reclining on the sofa.

"Fake I.D.," my father said, like he had one.

"No. We—me and other girls—wait outside the stage door for the band to show up. We carry in their stuff."

"What did you carry?" my father said, squinting.

"The microphone," I said, crying with relief.

Greg was the son my parents never had. They loved him and he loved them back. On the phone with my mother, I told her everything. "This doesn't change anything," she said. Which I kind of felt like it should.

With Trevor at home basking in the undivided attention of his grandparents, Greg and I parked in front of a three-story building near Yale. Descending a short flight of stairs was a shut door and a pair of sound machines in stereo. Our therapist, a mousy woman wearing small round glasses had an office that looked like it did double duty as a cabinet. Greg didn't just sit in a separate chair; he moved his chair an inch away, until it was against the wall. He blocked his view of me with his hand.

I was not the cause of our therapy sessions but I had shown up. My presence was an acknowledgment that I was willing to listen to the grievances against me. The expanse in our marriage seemed epic. My expectations of marriage were high, expectations I had been voicing since we met. Greg's expectations of me were high—although he never voiced them until now. I was supposed to be telepathic.

When Greg said to her, "I just don't know if I love her," I was silent the rest of the session and the drive home. This was essentially the same thing he'd said in our living room two months earlier, which I had dropped into the basement of my mind. But now he said it to someone else. This was a fracture that couldn't be ignored. A fracture cannot have space to grow into a chasm. Once my parents went home, I cornered Greg against the stove.

"You and me are leaving town."

"Where are we going?"

"I have no fucking clue." I had no fucking clue.

"I've always wanted to go to Maine."

"We're going to Maine." The last place I wanted to go was Maine.

He drove us to Maine the next weekend. We hugged the coast up route one in his pickup in a snowstorm. We had no place to stay. I hoped we'd find one. I hoped we'd find us.

We found an empty—but open—hotel by the ocean. In a spacious room on the middle floor with windows so wide it took two people to open the drapes. We made love for the first time in a month, for hours, in dim light.

On the drive home, Greg smiled and grabbed my hand. I unbuckled to sit next to him—to be closer. "We just—left." He said, motioning to the open road "We have to do that more."

"You can't work at the hospital anymore," I said.

He went into work the next day and quit. When he came home, he said that he walked into her—God, what was her name—office down the hall and told her that he would never see her again. "I adore my wife," he said.

At our final therapy appointment, Greg's chair touching mine, our hands entwined, the therapist asked what changed. Greg told her it was our drive to Maine. I knew he meant having sex in a hotel.

The first two definitions of *adore* require the subject to be a deity. The last definition is to regard with loving devotion. I'm no goddess. But devotion was good enough for me. I could build on that.

But first, I fled.

Hopping on a plane with my mother, on her dime, we visited my sister in Savannah where she was attending college. Leaving The South eleven years before, I hadn't been sorry to say goodbye to hair exploding humidity. I had missed snow. But I welcomed the heat. After a long winter at home, I sunk down in the back seat of our mother's rented Acura, relinquishing the front seat to my sister, my hand outside the window, playing with the Georgia breeze.

Languid, southern majesty was everywhere. In the two-hour breakfasts—*you want sweet tea or hot tea, darlin'?* In the Spanish moss. In the high-ceilinged antique store where I fingered a slightly damp Victorian chemise with handmade buttonholes. For a solid week I left my marriage to be right with myself.

When I returned, Greg had a new job with a private security firm. He had also built pantry shelves in an otherwise wasted closet. The way into my heart arrived via direct deposit and a tool belt. It wasn't just me who examined the fractures and worked to repair them. We were building again.

NINE

On my sixteenth birthday my mother drove me around Fairfax County to find me a job. "We're not going home until you have one," she said, gunning through a yellow light. "I can't afford your ballet addiction."

Until I'd run my index finger down the Yellow Pages, stopping at *Academy* because it was a word that signaled serious, I'd continued my Connecticut-learned ballet exercises at my mother's chipped kitchen counter, washing dishes with the supporting leg in a deep plié, opposite leg straight out from the hip, heel resting beside still soapy plates stacked on a dishtowel. When Madame Binda answered the phone, and I heard piano in the background, I knew I had found my place. "And," I told my mother, "she has an accent like Baryshnikov."

Madame taught wearing a long-sleeved black leotard pin-tucked between her generous breasts, a mid-calf black wrap skirt, black tights, black ballet slippers, and one of two black miniature poodles tucked under her arm. Madame did not show the steps. She said

them. In French. Her accent wasn't Russian like Mikhail Baryshnikov's, it was Belgian.

Gone were the five positions of the feet the way I knew them—in
English. First, second, third, fourth, and fifth were replaced with
première, deuxième, troisième, quatrième, and cinquième. Other
than merci beaucoup—which my sister and me had bastardized
into murky buttocks—I did not speak French. Baryshnikov had
flashy dimples. Madame did not smile. Madame assessed.

There was no place to hide in her studio, lined floor to ceiling
with mirrors, but I tried. Slipping between girls at the barre, I was
able to copy the girl in front of me no matter which direction we
faced. But during *centre*—variations danced away from the barre—I
shot to the back of the room. Like that old re-run episode of Lucille
Ball mirroring Harpo Marx that my grandmother loved, I became
a world class mimic.

A month before the end of the year performance—Madame
never said recital—she approached me after class. I gripped the
barre, wiping my forehead with a towel. I'd never seen her so close.
Her high cheekbones and upswept short black hair with shimmery
white strands seemed carved from marble. When she tilted her
head, a dangling pearl earring rested against the side of her throat.
Dark blue-gray eyes lined with kohl examined my face.

"It is time for you to move up, n'est-ce-pas?" One of her dark
arching eyebrows lifted to the heavens.

No.

I nodded.

There was a new girl, tall and skinny as real ballerinas were.

No matter how much salad and skinless chicken breasts I ate
and no matter how much my collar bones protruded, my hips
were there to stay. The victor in all my diet wars. But the new girl
needed to learn French. She also needed to stop farting anytime

Madame told her to lift her arms. The new, perfect-looking girl would move to the back.

"Your skin," Madame said, touching my cheek, "such *couleur*."

"I have my dead grandmother's skin," I spit out. "From Hungary."

Within an hour of leaving the house on my sixteenth birthday, I had a job at Ben Franklin, a crafts store. I made friends with the old ladies who worked in fabrics and ribbons. Until I met Eric. He was tan. And prince tall.

Our courtship began while learning to cashier. Counting back change, I always got flustered and had to fish the calculator from the pocket of my smock. Eventually, I placed the correct nickel or penny into a purse-lipped customer's impatient hand. When Eric made a mistake, he'd flash his neon smile and shrug. Correct change be damned.

I was assigned to Sewing. Eric to Framing. Eric found reasons to visit my department. After escorting a customer to the yarn aisle, or re-stocking an abandoned spool of thread, he'd loiter nearby and wait for me to notice. One night, just before closing, he leaned the wide dust mop against my workstation and said, "You know, in Oregon where I'm from, they call soda 'pop.'" He was seductive.

Our first date was sitting on the docks in Alexandria. He tilted my chin toward his, until my ponytail tickled my back, his lips a millimeter from mine and plucked a gray hair from my bangs like it was a crocus.

He taught me to waterski. Leaning against the edge of his family's speed boat, he slid off his Docksiders and into the skis. Behind my cheap sunglasses, I got a glimpse of his motivation in the gap between his thigh and bathing trunks.

Eric came to the Academy's performance. *He's out there*, I thought, twirling for my Prince of Picture Framing in my role as the Princess of Embroidery Floss in a bodice and full lace skirt, fake pearl tiara on my tightly bunned head. Driving me home, he pulled his car into my driveway, the floodlight over the garage blinding us. He leaned over the parking brake—*oh my God, it's happening*—his lips were soft, the car smelled like leather cleaner—I'd fantasized about this moment. His tongue eased my lips open; it was—

Bad. I broke away and jumped out of the car. My mother met me at the door holding a cup of tea. She wore her summer robe. She had a robe for every season. Summer meant floral print with crocheted ruffles at the neck and wrists. I followed her to the kitchen. She picked up the box of Kleenex from its spot next to the refrigerator and handed it to me.

"There's something wrong with me," I said, dropping into a chair. "If I had a brother and he kissed me, that's what it would have felt like." I pulled out a tissue, but no tears fell. They were caught in the full bottle of waterproof mascara ladled onto my eyelashes.

"There isn't a thing wrong with you," my mother said in the chair opposite. "He's just a boy." She handed me a Lorna Doone on a napkin. "You need a real man. Like a lumberjack."

Within my first week on the University of New Haven campus, I had a cafeteria routine. First, I'd pick my way to a small empty table to clean it and my seat with a wad of napkins. Second, I'd place my tray like a placemat on the opposite side for the no one who would be joining me. Third, I'd remove my tea and salad from the tray and position them perfectly. Salad without dressing—downstage. Tea with two tablespoons of sugar—stage left. I'd entwine my legs and drape a fresh napkin across my lap. Forking lettuce into my mouth, I chewed twenty times before swallowing. I knew exactly how I looked. In Virginia, I'd done this for years in front of my bedroom mirror.

In the months before we met, Greg watched. It should have been creepy. He told me about it as we lay naked on top of his single bed beneath a poster of California redwoods in the Delta Chi fraternity house.

Sitting in the cafeteria with his frat friends, they spied him checking me out.

"Dude," they laughed. "You couldn't get those legs apart with a crowbar." They dared him to talk to me.

Growing up the way he did, a boisterous kid in a boisterous house, Greg learned early to call dibs on the last pork chop on the platter. It should have been easy for him. Stand up, walk over, say hello to the virgin counting out her salad.

He discovered that I had a job at Koenig's art store in the mall on the way to buy himself a dangling spider earring for his left ear. Afterward, he sat on the orange vinyl bench opposite the art store watching me arrange Prismacolor markers while he smoked Marlboros.

One day, I passed the Delta Chi guys at their clothing drive table on the way to my volunteer job in the student run newspaper office. The guys egged him on. Put on some of these old clothes, they said. Go talk to her, they said.

These are the blanks he filled in later. All I saw when I looked up from the article I was proofreading was a tall, muscular guy in the doorway. He had lumberjack wrists. Grinning from ear to ear.

"Nice dress," I said.

Our first date was a week later—if a fraternity party counted as a date. I drove myself and parked on Westfield Street. I didn't need the address, Delta Chi House vibrated with the sound of heavy bass. The neighborhood was slammed together two and three family dwellings, each communing with the sidewalk, each with a chain-link fence. The fraternity house had dirty yellow aluminum siding. The door was flanked with metal trash cans. All the windows were fogged up. I held my breath, stepping over broken beer bottles, and opened the door to cigarette smoke and a Saint Bernard with a slice of sausage pizza in his mouth.

Light filtered down on a crush of bodies holding beer in Solo cups over their heads, moving room to room. Michael Stipe sang from a pair of four-foot-tall speakers *this one goes out to the one I've left behind.* I found the kitchen—gold brown linoleum, knotty pine cabinets, and a single frosted ceiling light with a flickering tubular bulb. It glowed blue. A card table was erected directly beneath the light. Two guys accepted red tickets and doled out cups. I approached the table, handed over my ticket, and was served a drink. "What is it?" I yelled into someone's ear.

"It's a kamikaze," he said. Everyone said. *A simple prop to occupy my time.* Everything happened in unison. Young women wearing acid wash jeans and unwashed hair, jumping off sofa arms into the laps of dudes in red and gold satin fraternity jackets. I wore Hollywood waist pants, a black silk blouse with a brooch, huge earrings, kitten heels, and a significant quantity of liquid black eyeliner—for confidence.

I'd eaten a butternut donut that morning. It was eleven at night. One kamikaze led to another, refilled by a graduate student who was the R.A. in the freshman dorm. The Cell Block they called it. *That's me in the corner, that's me in the spotlight.* The flyer for the party was in my purse. I fought the urge to look at it, to confirm that Greg had invited me.

I was about to leave when I saw him—a head above everyone else. Red hair, broad shoulders, tidy hips. And then he was in front of me. And then he took my hand, lead me out of the kitchen, my kitten heels sticking to dried beer.

"Do you want to see the house?" He said, like fraternity house tours were a thing.

"Yes."

He cleared a path through elbows and feet up the carpeted staircase, to the end of the tour. His room. It was very neat. His bed, the bottom half of a bunkbed from home, was covered with a red afghan with little balls knitted to the surface. He took my plastic kamikaze cups—somehow, I had two—and placed them on his tall dresser. And we danced. *Losing my religion.* He was tall, earnest, trim, really liking me, holding me, wanting me—and I was short, buzzed, kissing him—starving.

We got married the fall after graduation.

I was Interior Design and he was Criminal Justice.

TEN

If anyone had asked me at nineteen as I dipped my calligraphy nib into India ink, tracing the nude figure drawing model's curves with my eyes—blind to what my hand was doing—what my life would look like in four years, I would have gestured to my paper and said *this*.

Halfway through my sophomore year, my mother held a family meeting with my sister and me. Our father was at work. Heather was there as a witness, since all the money tossed in the center of the table was mine. Birthday bonds from my great-grandmother that my mother kept in a small metal box with a key, were covered by a handful of Susan B. Anthony dollars and silver half-dollars I'd squirrelled away in the top drawer of my bureau, inside one of my baby shoes.

I re-registered as a part-time student and took a summer temp job at an insurance office, ignorant to its permanence. I filed manila folders with color-coded stickers, answered a fifty-button phone that never stopped ringing, and greeted walk-in customers carrying cash to buy insurance cards for barely running cars in order to get to work again after losing their license to successive DWIs.

One day as a temp in shorts became ten years as a full-time, fully licensed property and casualty agent in a bargain rack suit. In the beginning, the money paid for college. Then it paid for half of our wedding. Then it paid for half of our mortgage, daycare, and Greg's graduate school. I was a Valley girl, even if I didn't live in the Valley anymore. Valley girls are advised by their Valley fathers to keep good jobs and keep them for life.

By the time Greg and I were rebuilding our marriage, I'd left the first insurance office for another—but the gig was the same. I balanced file folders on my head, one leg extended, tip of my high heel pointed, while speaking to customers on the phone and signing papers. Having a job where I could check out mentally and still perform came in handy when my personal life was in free fall—like now.

It was during a lunch break, driving back from errands to the office when I felt the tightening—like an elastic band—on the left side of my abdomen. Everything stilled—even as I drove fifty miles an hour on a divided highway in Wallingford. The church we married in a mile away. I replayed a singular scene like a movie. The substitute minister—ours was travelling out of the country and forgot to tell us—kept addressing me and repeating the bountiful blessing of having many children, like it was an order. I'd wanted to laugh in his face. I did a U-turn into the drugstore parking lot.

Peeing on the stick in the office bathroom, I divined a perfect result. I would be better. A better mother for a start—I'd breast feed until the baby went to college. A better wife—we'd have sex immediately after delivery right in the maternity ward. He would forget what's her name. I would forget what's her name. We would be a family. I beamed from the toilet. At home, I showed Greg the white plastic wand with the pink plus sign in the window and he said *fuck.*

ELEVEN

It was a bright day in May when I began bleeding. All the windows were open, the sweet smell of lilac breezing through the house. I sat at our dining room table paying the bills. When I stood up to walk to the mailbox, a rush of heat came from between my legs. My face and arms were cold. Squeezing my butt cheeks together, sitting on a bloody towel, I called Dr. Robb.

Lying on the white papered table, I tried to relax my thighs and ass so he could insert the internal ultrasound wand into my vagina. Greg and I stared at the miniscule monitor, expecting nothing. Five years earlier, before Trevor, I'd begun miscarrying in a cheap Rhode Island hotel. We made it home to our West Haven apartment before I allowed the eight-week-old pregnancy to end. It slipped out of me, clotted brown blood mixing with Tidy Bowl and gone in seconds.

On the ultrasound monitor, where we expected nothing, there was something. A small jellybean pulsing inside a bubble. I felt no relief when Dr. Robb said, "Things are fine," or when Greg grabbed my hand, his green eyes wet. My heart had stopped. Long after the monitor was turned off, I stared at the blank screen wishing back evidence of life, of a beating heart that could shock mine into action.

At the end of August, my mother and I went to Newport, a brief Rhode Island getaway weekend for the two of us. There had been no more bleeding incidents and I had finally stopped running to the bathroom to check my underwear every hour. The sun was high, and I liked the way the short-sleeved striped maxi dress I wore clung to my skin and exposed my belly. We strolled along Bellevue Avenue. The waveless First Beach lifted me into a state of calm. It wasn't the bargaining calm I'd felt when I discovered I was pregnant so soon after Greg's affair. I'd realized pretty quickly that the pregnancy was not a balm for our marriage, it was a balm only for me. I'd been feeling the baby kick for a couple of months and when it kicked as I stood on the sidewalk in front of a baby boutique, I pulled my mother inside.

Everything was soft, even the walls. Pale iced pinks and quiet watery blues, muted versions of the colors outside. A bowl of pastel pacifiers resembled butter mints. The blankets were downy, terrycloth towels with rabbit-ear hoods were supple. Nothing bad is allowed to happen in a baby boutique.

Standing at the portal of maternal sanctuary and its cool understated baby glamour, I opened my mouth and swallowed the boutique whole. The soft pill dissolved and spread, causing temporary amnesia. I forgot the affair, that I had lost a baby, and the fear that I would lose the baby I carried. I forgot to fear for my marriage. I digested. I wanted to buy everything in the store. Everything was a single ivory cable-knit newborn baby bunting with a hood and invisible zipper. I held my belly—it would be a girl—and forked over my credit card to the saleswoman, the ticket to bringing my $125.00 fantasy home with me.

"Oh! You must be due soon," she said, eyeing my bump while wrapping the bunting in a box with gold-flecked tissue.

"Um. No, not until January." My mother and I left the store laughing that I would be giving birth to an Amazon.

At home was a message. Lab results from routine pregnancy blood tests said that my baby was sick. There were two possibilities: Spina Bifida or Anencephaly. Either our baby had a damaged spine or a damaged brain. "It isn't possible," I told Dr. Robb on the late Sunday night phone call. "I feel this baby moving all the time."

Two days later, me, Greg, and my mother were at Yale Hospital—not my usual hospital—in a room the size of a banquet hall. Inside were four items: a gurney, ultrasound equipment, a movie screen, and a bench. It was dark. I settled myself on the gurney. The expressionless technician held a lubricated wand on my belly and told us to watch the screen. I watched the technician instead. At his hard lips, at how he chewed them. At the tattoo of an anchor on his forearm. "Look at the screen," he said again.

I turned to the screen. There were two egg shaped circles magnified to Godzilla proportions. *I'm having a mutant.* The technician said something.

"What?" I said.

"Did you have an ultrasound before?"

"Yes, at two months." *A jumping jellybean.*

"What did they tell you?"

The scream came from someplace deep. "What's wrong with my baby!"

"There is nothing wrong with your baby. There's two of them. Would you like to know the sex?"

No. I didn't ever want to have sex again.

"Mrs. Kalafus?"

"We're going to wait." I wanted the surprise of a daughter. Daughters.

From the bench my mother screamed "Twins! What are they?"

"I guess we want to know," I said, giving in. I could have earned a PhD in giving in.

The technician—still unsmiling—moved the wand over my belly like a rover on the surface of the moon.

"This one is clearly a boy. And this one—this one is a boy too."

My mother had insisted on coming. "Who will be there for Greg if he's there for you?" she'd said. She left the bench and ran to the movie screen. "It's the most beautiful thing I've ever seen in my life," she said and burst into tears.

I wasn't thinking about boys or girls. I was trying to remember the bumper sticker I'd seen recently on a Honda Odyssey. *Minivans are evidence that hell exists.* I decided to say something intelligent.

"Are they conjoined?"

The anchor in the technician's arm flexed. He removed his wand and scowled at me. "That is extremely rare. I can't tell if they are fraternal or identical, they're too big. You'll know once they're born."

What if they are ten pounds each I wanted to ask. I saw myself on *Oprah*, pulling my babies on set in a wagon because they were too heavy to hold. I twisted my head to see Greg sitting alone on the bench. Stress can debilitate or motivate. He didn't eat or speak for two days.

For the next few months my hair was lush and my breasts grew to peasant-sized proportions. I could have fed the nation. I tended to everything at once: Trevor, my job, Greg, and the cut-glass doorknobs. Polishing them became a hobby. I was a goddess with a houseful of crystal balls, power emanating from my belly.

I should have been ready. But as my mid-January due date approached, fear did too. Late one night, searching the internet for information on twins, I fell on divorce statistics. The third largest group of divorced couples were those where either spouse was a police officer. The runner up was if one of those officers had shot someone. First prize for largest divorce percentages were parents of multiples. I searched statistics, any statistics, on marriages where the husband had an affair and the wife fell pregnant with twins. The computer delivered a blank screen.

TWELVE

Nightmares have a commonality: a real event is magnified, swollen by unconsciousness. My body in pregnancy was heavier and therefore hungrier. Late at night, the moon shining on the landing of the staircase, my feet in thick socks creaking on each oak tread, I sneaked into the kitchen. Sugar Smacks. Cocoa Pebbles. Whole Milk. Mixing them together with my spoon, I cradled the bowl, savoring my taboo. Leaning against the street facing double windows, I brushed against the fine linen swags and jabots I'd sewn. Knife edge pleats.

I left the lights off to look out, undetected. The darkness soothed. The inactivity of my neighbors, lack of traffic, the yard too dark to make a mental list of chores. Trim the forsythia. Hack the poison ivy climbing up the pine at the root. Chocolate flakes and sugar-coated puffed wheat filled my cheeks. The milk in the bowl turned from light to dark. Past our green-black front yard, in the illumination of a single streetlight, I saw someone. It had to be another drunk college kid walking up from the bar.

I banged my forehead against the cold glass to get a better look. It was a woman. She leaned forward, negotiating the steep hill. Her arms were crossed in front of her chest. Then, clarity. An unprocessed slip of film in the darkroom dipped into a bath of developer. Watching her feline movements, I swallowed the soggy ball in my mouth. The moon hid behind a cloud. Only parts of her shone in the streetlight. A band of gold around her neck. Fangs. The thickness of her leg muscles and sharpness of her shoulder blades were masterful—a horror. She twitched and turned, prowling all night, up and down our street.

Backing away from the window, I left the bowl on the table and ran upstairs not caring if the stairs creaked. I got into bed and curled against Greg's back.

In the morning, there was no bowl of half-eaten cereal. There was only the memory of sugar in my mouth, a knot in my gut, and of being between worlds. I knew what I saw. The creature—part woman, part panther—was the woman Greg had the affair with. And she wanted to kill me.

THIRTEEN

The nightmare didn't reveal her name. A . . . something. I was certain. But what about the rest?

AnaAliceAmandaAndreaAbagailAliciaAdrienneAprilAnnAmbrosia

No. What I could remember was that she wasn't thin. I filled in the rest: fuller, wider, hairier, lustier. They'd fucked at her place. She'd asked him to come over and do some handyman work. I imagined a female Big Foot holding a broken lightbulb.

In counseling there had been a lot of push and pull. The little red flag in the middle of the rope was labeled *more*. Greg wanted more sex. I wanted more conversation. Counseling must have worked; I was pregnant, wasn't I? He was proving his devotion by being devoted, wasn't he? If I didn't get everything I wanted, I dealt with it. Who gets everything anyway? I called the boutique in Newport and had them ship me another over-priced baby bunting.

To be fair, Greg tried to understand my interests. After sex we talked. Mostly, I talked. He held off sleep until it became too much. I knew now that promises in therapy were the tip of another fairy tale. If I wanted something, I would have to make it happen, not wait for it to be handed to me like a wedding gift. So I didn't stretch my creative muscles the way I had stretched my legs at the barre—or charcoal in hand, skimmed across a wide sheet of paper, smearing from pinky to wrist.

Ballet classes were a distant memory. The last thing I drew was a floor plan of a do-it-ourselves kitchen remodel on a paper towel with an indelible laundry marker. I had to live in the present. I had a choice, be resentful about what I couldn't make or focus on what I was in the process of making.

I tried to convince myself it was enough. Ripples of betrayal became a tsunami biddable with my fingertip when Greg called from his new office and said he'd be late.

I was in the kitchen, cracking eggs into a bowl. Whisking them, I added milk, salt and pepper, moving them around the pan with a wooden spatula at high heat. Transferring them to a plastic bowl with a suction cupped bottom for Trevor's supper.

When Trevor was born, I was intimidated. At twenty-six, despite a lengthy pre-teen career as a babysitter, I was ill-prepared to be in a hospital recovery room, hear an infant scream in the hallway and know that he was mine. When the nurse placed him in my arms, all I could think was how Dr. Robb had said not to have sex for a month after my miscarriage. We waited a week. When I phoned Dr. Robb about still not having my period six weeks after the miscarriage telling him that my breasts were still sore and I wanted to vomit at the sight of a tuna fish can, he said *if it walks like a duck and talks like a duck—it's a duck.*

Trevor did not look like a duck. His pink eyelids and mouth opened at the same time. They needed things from me, they couldn't wait for me to get my shit together.

"What do I do?" I said to the nurse.

She reached over, opened my johnnie coat and exposed my left breast. With the same adeptness that allowed her to carry newborn infants around like restaurant platters, she squeezed my breast and pushed Trevor's head toward it. When the pinch from his mouth came, my own mouth opened and I recoiled into the pillow.

"It's OK," she said, leaving, "this is normal."

Nothing felt less normal. A lactation expert visited me. I couldn't figure out how to get Trevor to latch on, every time I attempted, I failed, I told her. The lactation consultant picked him up and inserted her index finger into his mouth.

"Hmm," she said, removing her finger. "This may complicate things. His frenulum is short." Then she handed him back to me like a loaf of ill-baked bread.

"What does that mean?" I looked at Trevor's perfectly shaped mouth.

"The frenulum is a bit of tissue that connects the tongue to the throat. His is short and he might be harder than most babies to nurse."

I didn't have most babies. I only had this one. The tricks began. The consultant held a bottle of sugar water over my breast, dribbling it onto the nipple. I learned a variety of baby holds. The Football Hold. The Lateral Hold. I considered hanging myself from the ceiling and trying it that way.

No one was with me when my milk came in. The consultant was at the hospital, not our apartment. Trevor was sleeping in his bassinet under the living room window to reduce his slight jaundice. Greg ran out to get coffee. I was in the bedroom, trying to pull on a bra over my rock-hard breasts. I went to the mirror. The skin on my breasts was taught and pink. Veins had appeared. Originating at my neck, they bypassed my collar bones, like rivers, branching off in two different directions with similar destinations. Left breast. Right breast. A droplet of white peeked out from each nipple.

I had everything I needed to get things right: baby, breast, milk. Trevor screamed. Greg came home and paced the hall. The hospital had given us free samples of ready-to-drink formula. Greg poured the formula into a bottle and handed it to me. Trevor sucked the bottle dry.

I arranged for a breast pump from the visiting nurse. The first time I attached its yellow cone to my breast, I was mesmerized by the whish-whish-whish as the cone pulled my nipple, sucking and releasing while milk streamed out. In minutes I filled a nine-ounce bottle. I quickly changed sides. Whish-whish-whish. With plastic, I had done it.

I'd experienced migraine headaches off and on since I was eighteen. An aura of vibrating fuzz would shield my vision and I would need to drop everything and lie down in a dark room. After an hour or four of writhing in pain, I would fly out of bed and vomit in the toilet. It was the only time my high energy was flattened. On birth control, the migraines came more frequently. Just after we married, I was prescribed Cafergot. One pill at the onset of an aura, and a half a pill every hour until there was no pain. It worked—most of the time.

I was handing a customer her insurance card when an aura showed up. I took a pill and went back to signing insurance cards. The pain shot across my head. Another pill. When the phone rang at my desk, I tried to answer it but I couldn't move my arm. I opened my mouth at the ringing phone. No words came out.

My coworker phoned Greg. By the time I was seen in the emergency room, I'd thrown up in the bathroom twice and would have sold my mother for a hamburger. I'd had a hemiplegic migraine. The symptoms mirror a stroke. I went off birth control. If migraines were a nuisance without a newborn, with a newborn, migraines were an impossibility. Cafergot was a belladonna.

Atropa belladonna was named by Carl Linnaeus, a Swedish botanist who was the father of binomial nomenclature—the formal system of naming organisms. Each name consists of two parts, the genus and the specific. Belladonna—*beautiful woman* in Italian—was selected as a reference to the antiquated practice of dropping juice from the plant's berries into the eyes in order to dilate the pupils, supposedly making a woman appear more seductive. Atropa was a reference to Atropos, one of the Three Fates of Greek mythology. Also known as the Moirai, these three sisters personified life—the destiny of each mortal—as thread on a spindle. Clotho spun the thread. Lachesis measured it out. Atropos cut it.

Belladonnas have a long history for use as both medicine and poison. I couldn't nurse—or pump—and take it. I also couldn't have a debilitating migraine and take care of my infant. I kept the pills and switched to formula. My mother was disappointed. She told me often how satisfying nursing had been. She told me again on the drive to Macy's, Greg at home with Trevor, so I could buy a new outfit and return to work. I couldn't afford to stay home. *Maybe I'm not mother material*, I thought. Not in the way of good women with swaddled children wrapped to their chests. They were happy, it seemed, not minding the weight gain, taking it all in stride being more natural. I mean, weren't they always eating bananas? After my mother threw in the towel on nutrition, I grew up on Velveeta. I envied those natural women. I was not one of them.

Fingering a silk blouse in Macy's, my breasts pulsed. I ran to the fancy ladies' lounge, looked around—for I didn't know what—ran to the sink, pulled down my top and squeezed, expressing milk into the sink. In the stall behind me, a woman was urinating. We expressed together.

Running water into the crusty egg pan, I turned off the faucet, and leaving the phone where Greg had just said he would be late on the floor where I tossed it, I shuffled to the sunroom. Trevor sat at a pint-sized table watching cartoons. Kneeling in front of him, I scooped up a spoonful of eggs. His lips were slightly closed—resting. I touched the space between his lips and he blew eggs all over my face.

I don't remember removing him from his chair. I don't remember climbing the stairs. I remember my arms straight out, holding his strong four-year-old body away from me, his arms and legs dangling. I remember dropping him on his bed, pivoting to the doorway, and pivoting back. Trevor sat stunned on his bed. I didn't lose eye contact when I slammed the door shut. He screamed and cried and I did not care. I lumbered down the stairs to the kitchen, forgot why I was there and lumbered back to the sunroom. Bits of egg were all over the floor. I sat down in the toddler chair and ate the cold eggs remaining in the bowl.

Upstairs, Trevor was still crying when I reached for the doorknob to his room. I tried to turn it. It didn't budge. I wiggled it. The crying stopped.

"Mom?" I heard his feet jump to the floor.

"Trevor, open the door."

The doorknob jiggled.

"It won't open. I'm going to be stuck in here forever!"

We eyed each other through the keyhole.

"I'll be right back," I told him.

The house only had two doors that locked from the inside: the master bedroom and the bathroom. The other rooms lacked the oval brass locking knob that curved toward the door like a horizontal letter C. The only way to lock these doors was the way you unlocked them—with a key. I had slammed the door so hard the internal locking lever fell. Downstairs, I went to the pre-Civil War bureau I inherited and slid open the top drawer. There it was—the plug for my tsunami—the skeleton key for the sunroom Ann mailed me resting on a piece of green felt.

When I inserted the key in the keyhole of Trevor's door, it opened.

FOURTEEN

A woman says, "She's waking up." It is a sweet voice. The sweetest voice I've ever heard. If I open my eyes, I can see who she is, but my eyes are frozen shut. Someone is stroking my forehead. There are beeps.

"Is that her temperature?"

My mother. How did my mother get here?

"You're doing great, Chris."

My father. How did my father get here?

Where am I?

"Let's warm her up," says the sweet-voiced woman. Two sounds: crinkly like tissue paper and one like the furnace of a hot air balloon. I'm defrosting. I open my eyes into slits. The stainless-steel pendant light overhead is off. I am covered with an inflatable tin foil blanket.

"There she is!" The sweet voice is a nurse. She writes something on a chart. She turns off machines. It's just her, me, my mother and father. My father is the one stoking my forehead. My favorite scene in the *Wizard of Oz* is when Dorothy wakes up in her own bed.

It was just a nightmare. See? We got blown around, but everyone's the same. Auntie Em, Uncle Henry, Professor Marvel—the farm hands. My own hands are free and roam under the tin foil blanket. I touch my belly and breast. Bandages. I can't remember why. Before I can ask I'm wheeled out of the room and into the hallway.

My mother's mother, Grandma Eva is here. Aunts, uncles, my in-laws, Alison—Greg, who is crying. We form a strange parade. I'm the float that everyone else walks behind. I am parked in a room with a huge window. Flurries of nurses float around my family, pinning stuff to a corkboard wall. One shows me a button. "Morphine," she says. Two transparent plastic bassinets are rolled in. Inside each one is a sleeping baby.

My mother swoops. I am mechanically raised to a slightly reclined position. Navigating tubes and surgical tape, my mother places a baby in each of my flaccid arms. I want to ask *whose babies are these* but my lips won't move. I feel drunk so I must be drunk. My mother stands at the end of the hospital bed with a camera.

"Smile!"

I think I am smiling, but when she shows me the screen, it's only my top lip, curling.

Classic.

I look down at the babies. Their eyes are squeezed shut and their bodies are wrapped like mummies. I try to smile again, but my mouth feels full of gauze like when I had my wisdom teeth pulled. I'm probably drooling. I lower my face to each of the babies and sniff. Baby smell. *Jesus Christ, these are my babies.* Double baby smell is more like laughing gas than Novocain. But I guess I don't look happy. Alison, veteran mother and professional baby minder, gets close to the bed and looks me over.

"You look like hell," she says. Turning to the room, she says, "Everybody out—let's go people!" like a bouncer in a bar at 2 AM. Alison is blonde, tiny, and favors bohemian skirts and silver bracelets. Everyone, except Greg, leaves—including my mother. Alison pulls up the rear, scanning the room for stragglers. Seeing none, she flashes me the peace sign and walks out, pulling the wide metal door shut with a click.

The year I turned six, I developed tonsillitis. The fever always visited at night. I would be sound asleep in my twin bed when delirium took over. The doorknob on my closet would turn and the door would rotate open. Gone was the hollow-core sandalwood slab. It was replaced by a solid black revolving door. Commence the ride! The Partition of Terror! Frankenstein's Monster, the Mummy, the Wicked Witch of the West, and Dracula revolved slowly, swiping at me but held in place by cemented shoes.

When I screamed, my mother rushed in, bedroom door slamming into the closet, trapping the monsters. Throwing back my blanket and sheets, I was gathered up, my arms around her neck, my owl pajamas soaked with sweat. Her lips on my forehead. I was being burned from the inside. A cold-water bath until my jaw shook.

After weeks of feverish temperatures, hives from penicillin, and after my tonsils were removed, I told her what I'd seen. How after the bath that killed the monsters, a hole appeared in the ceiling in my bedroom like the opening of a panoramic Easter egg. The attic was full of bicycles. My escape hatch had wheels.

Years later she told me that I'd never said the word "monster."

"You said 'the factories' were coming for you. I figured you meant the hospital. You were scared to death of the hospital."

A nurse enters the room. She carefully removes Spencer and Parker from my arms and places them in their Lucite bassinets. She pulls the drapes closed. Greg is asleep in a chair. It's mid-morning but I've delivered two six-pound babies and a tumor. The day is over.

77

I'm in my hospital room. Alone. There are no beeping machines or tinfoil blankets. I have no tubes. Just smooth linoleum tiles and fully opened drapes bracketing the evening sky.

For the last four days, I've been a carnival attraction. Twins and breast cancer are too tempting to pass by. Doctors who are not mine stop in to check me out. Not to see me—to investigate me. Tiptoeing in, peeling back a bandage while my eyes are closed. Greg sent one particular student doctor packing. But the trickster hid, tucking into a doorway until Greg left. The trickster reappeared, a small man at my bed. He was reaching toward my breast repeating a version of what they all said *I'm just here to check on you.* My right hand became a guillotine. *Slap.* He left, not looking me in the eye, but longingly at my johnnie coat.

Tomorrow I will go home—if I urinate. The morphine drip has reduced my voice to a hum. I'd been blurry since the surgeries. Now, morphine free, I see myself clearly. Stuck in a room, in a hospital, in a city—the world. My world is a bed on wheels and a bathroom. No leaving until I urinate. Successful urination will grant me the winning ticket to sleeplessness, bottle feedings, doctor appointments, solving the mystery of clandestine cancer, and all the wrong clothes in my closet.

I consider lying. Maybe I don't remember how to pee. I think of my cousin Amy. She delivered her ten-pound daughter without an epidural and the next day slipped into a size three gold jumper from high school and went home. On my food tray is the remote for the T.V. I turn it on and a floating head appears. The head speaks.

"I don't know what challenges you face, but I know you can do it."

It's God. He's looking into my soul. A name flashes at the bottom of the screen.

Tony Robbins.

In Virginia, there was a televangelist whose program I saw flipping between *This Old House* and *Not Necessarily the News.* The powerful Black preacher had his congregants on their knees. One by one, he slapped his palm on their foreheads. *You're saved.*

Saved is a red button with immediate access to a floor full of qualified baby minders. Mine for one more night. Mine before the flood comes. Greg and Trevor are at home. For this last night in the hospital, I ask that the twins spend it in the nursery.

FIFTEEN

I stand in the dark. We have been home for one day—not even twenty-four hours yet. I need to understand my body's new post-op language. I need to feel that I am safe. I need to return to the house that I used to think of as my tea-kettle fortress—no matter what the neighborhood kids call it.

The moon coming in through the arch of the bathroom window over the toilet and the soft glow of the lampshade covered nightlight are my company. The built-in linen closet is at my back. The linen closet doors, even if you push, never close properly. Towels, sheets, tub toys—I'm forever reaching into this closet. Seventy-seven years and what could be just as many layers of off-white paint means that every time I open the doors, or just pass by them, I try to close the damn doors. Tonight, they rest in peace. I lean back and let them support me. I exhale and the whole house relaxes.

I navigated successfully to the bathroom, but now I can't remember the pattern of quiet floorboards. Moving from this spot means creaking and creaking is the trigger that shoots off Parker wailing which makes Spencer wail—the whole Rube Goldberg horror machine. Not moving means I can be alone. I haven't been alone in years.

The house in early January contracts but doesn't constrict. The oak floorboards pull into themselves and invite me to do the same. In the cradle of my house, I have the urge to sway. Although I am wrapped in bandages, a tank top, two crew neck shirts, two pairs of socks, and pajama bottoms, I am freezing.

After Grandma Rose died, I came to own the pajamas she wore in the hospital. Thin combed cotton of the palest blue, they had a drawstring. I wore them for years. They were my period pajamas. I wore them well after the weave in the fabric loosened. When I walked, they pooled around my ankles. The hems frayed and the blood stains in the crotch wouldn't completely disappear, but I kept wearing them. I wish I still had them.

The burst of tears I still haven't shed is an icicle between my ribs, sharp as a swallowed hiccup. To keep it there, I press the heels of my hands to my eyes. That hiccup is going to have to come out. If it stays in, it will result in a wound that will not heal. Although, it may be too late.

The surgeon removed the tumor from my chest, but no one knows if cancer has colonized my brain, liver, or lungs. Removing my hands from my eyes, I wrap my arms around my flabby mid-section. If I unleash the hiccup the wrought iron chandelier I had to have in that cozy as fuck store will sway. The natural spring beneath our house will become a geyser and the walls will crumble—because I will have said the unsayable. I will have laid the blame for my disease, in all its watery hell, at the feet of my husband.

I know that Greg is in the waiting room of the hospital. I know that I am here to have a battery of tests. I don't know what time it is, where we parked, or how to get back to the waiting room once I come out of this CT scan tube. It's a sensation of forgetting that is exactly like losing my place on the highway. Lulled by the vibration of tires on pavement and uniform grass in the median, I would snap to consciousness somewhere between exit signs on I 95 or the Merritt Parkway.

If it happened on the Merritt, I'd be on the lookout for the bridge with the two pairs of cement angel wings until cresting a hill, the West Rock tunnel in the distance and realize I'd missed it.

The tunnel goes through the body of Maushop. Maushop wasn't as lucky as his twin brother Hobbomock, the Sleeping Giant, in his eternal landscape nap. Originally from Cape Cod, both Native giants guarded a sacred mound where tribute to Thunder and Morning Star was made, until they had a fight with the thunderbirds.

While his brother was put to sleep, Maushop heaved his body up a tree. Giants are hard to hide. Especially giants who eat whales they catch with their hands. The thunderbirds brought a flood. They aimed their bolts at the tree. Maushop fell from the tree, drowned, and became Mautumpseck, *bad rock place*.

Before I knew the legend, I approached the tunnel thinking it looked like a woman lying on her side. I get lost on highways, but not with my body. I know exactly where on my waist my forearm likes to rest; just below where my hip arches toward the sky. My opposite arm stretches across the floor, supporting my head above my ear while I watch *The Bachelor*, or read *People* magazine.

Northbound, you enter the tunnel in New Haven and exit in Hamden.

Northbound, you enter the tunnel below a dip in the rock, at her womb.

I don't have to worry about the way back. Once the CT scan is done, I am led to another room for an x-ray of my lungs followed by a Muga scan—a diagnostic tool for the heart. I am led room by room by a shepherdess. Arm here. Leg there. This will pinch. Mind the lever.

My shepherdess leaves me at the entrance for the MRI. She has to guide her children home from daycare. The MRI technician is very young and pretty. I smooth my johnnie coat like it is a Diane von Furstenberg wrap dress.

"You need to lie face down on the table. Take the coat off," she says, pointing to a metal peg on the wall.

There are two holes on the table, one for each of my breasts. I tell her I don't know if I can do it. "My sutures might come undone. I just gave birth last week."

She shrugs. "So, take your time."

I slip off the johnnie coat. I feel her eyes on my pouchy stomach and scarred breast. She offers no assistance. I'm positioning my breasts into the holes when she leaves me for the observation room—away from the radiation—and pushes a button. The C-section sutures hold, but the rest of me doesn't. I cry and stream milk all over the base of the MRI machine while high-pitched pinging ricochets in my ears. Next is the brain scan where I am given contrast dye intravenously. The dye makes me radioactive. I'm told not to hold or touch my children for twenty-four hours.

The body scan is a different day. All work and no play makes Jack a dull boy. All scans and no break makes Jane disassociate. Greg must return to work. I'm not allowed to drive; my mother will take me.

My father has two brothers and it is their wives my mother recruits to hold the twins while she and I are on our hospital outing. Aunt Barbara is tall and quiet. Aunt Marti is short and chatty. They have five grown children between them. I have arrived at a place where I worry about nothing. There is probably a scan for that.

How I remember the Radiology Department is incorrect. I remember it directly next to the Sisters of Charity Gift Shoppe where *it's a boy* and *it's a girl* metallic balloons are sold. Buildings are condensed to a single room. It feels like this: you fall asleep in a chair at your kitchen table and wake up in Radiology sitting in a yellow orange molded plastic chair. Next, you notice the blue diamond patterned carpet and that the whole place looks new, updated since the day before, and completely nonthreatening, like Ikea.

The waiting room in Radiology is crowded, with no two seats together. My mother sits diagonally from me, feet planted firmly on the ground, both hands gripping her black leather handbag. I am at the end of an aisle of old people who face another aisle of old people. Everyone seems separated from who came with them. I look for facial similarities between rows, like elementary school worksheets where you draw a line between an apple and pie or a bird and a nest. That fully bearded man with that puffy faced woman. The two bald men in Patagonia jackets. The easiest one is last. A solid broad line from my mother to me. Her Naturalizer lace-up soft soled shoe to my faux leather mule. When I'm done, an invisible crisscrossed trip line covers the floor.

My mother tucks her handbag behind the small of her back, leaning forward to position it. *Drink it* she mouths at me. I'm six years old and we're at the kitchen sink in Beacon Falls. She holds a transparent bottle of mineral oil and pours it into a spoon. I'd discovered that I was capable of holding my bowels and decided I would never poop again. I clamp my mouth to the spoon.

"You don't want to end up in the hospital again, do you?"

The tonsillectomy was still fresh. Their pediatric ward with rows of oversized baby cribs was even fresher. I opened my mouth and swallowed.

I'm not six. I'm thirty-one. A child-mother. A mother-child.

In my hands is an opaque white plastic bottle of barium. I must drink the entire bottle so the machinists in the factory will know if there is cancer hiding in my body. Like Alice falling down the rabbit hole aching to be shut up like a telescope to fit through a tiny door. *Drink me.* She did. I can't make myself swallow this liquid magnifying glass.

My mother and I used to play Hide and Seek. I always chose her closet to hide in. It was dark and quiet. Only the sound of my own breathing, soft from toddler lips. I hid behind my mother's bright flowered dresses, a polyester hothouse of yellow and orange zinnias. I'd nestle between them, becoming a flower. My bare toes were lit by streaming sun, a slim rectangle reaching beneath the sliding birch door.

I'm going to find you she'd call from the living room. Then the light rectangle disappeared and the door rushed open and there she was—my beautiful mother—back-lit, brown hair parted on the side and falling in a bouncy flip at her shoulders. Her hair fell forward when she bent to pick me up. I leapt into her arms.

I still hold the barium. There's a straw sticking out of the mouth of the bottle. The barium has been refrigerated but it tastes like chalk. I place the straw between my lips and sip so slowly my mother begins to laugh. "She's never been good about milkshakes," she says to the woman next to her. It isn't true. In high-school, lunch was a milkshake. I'd leave the cafeteria for the faculty parking lot and sit on the curb scooping the thick chocolate shake with a spoon. It was the only thing at that school that was edible. That and French fries. Sometimes, I'd ditch the spoon and use a trio of fries instead.

I've been given an hour to drink the barium. The receptionist holds up a kitchen timer. I have fifteen minutes. Everyone watches. The man with the bushy beard watches. One half of the Patagonia pair is in with the doctor, the other half pretends to read a magazine, but he's watching. I watch my mother. She shakes her head. The receptionist gives me a ten-minute warning.

"What happens if she doesn't drink it?" the woman next to my mother asks her.

"We'll have to reschedule and come back," my mother says to her, but looking at me.

There's a sensation of the walls closing in. A desire to step on the gas. I once read that people hit their brakes in tunnels because speed is hard to discern without trees. Enter the tunnel and there is a tiny light at the end, far away and then, suddenly, it's not. It's very, very close.

Time to fly. I stand while making like I'm sucking the barium down, pretending to swallow. I hold the barium hostage inside the straw with the consistent suction of my tongue. I catch my mother's eye, lifting a pinkie off the barium, motioning to the bathroom as I walk there.

Inside, I look at myself in the mirror over the sink. The straw is still between my teeth. Releasing the straw, I tilt the bottle to read it. There are no words, like *drink me* or *one hundred percent more effective than other barium brands*, just a black line illustration of a stomach. I peek in the mouth of the bottle. I've finished half of it. Holding my gaze in the mirror, I take the straw out of the bottle, place it between my teeth like a matador, and dump the remaining barium down the drain.

When the technician says, "Did you finish the bottle?"

"Absolutely," I say.

She pushes the button and I slide into the tube.

SIXTEEN

When I unglue my eyelashes, I recognize my living room. I fell asleep sitting up. Raising my head, I realize my mouth is hanging wide open and I close it. The yellow and white afghan is over my legs. Grandma Rose knitted it for me when my mother was pregnant with my sister. I was moved from the smaller bedroom, to the larger one opposite my parents' room. My mother painted it butter yellow and hung matching yellow and white gingham curtains on the windows. My mother must have found the afghan in the back of the linen closet. I hear her in my kitchen on the phone. That old clunky cordless model that I'd been meaning to replace.

When Greg and I toured the house before making our asking-price offer, I noticed a long slender door in one of the walls of the small kitchen. Lifting the latch revealed a built-in ironing board, warped from steam. On the back written in pencil were the heights of the children who had been raised here. I don't iron. I throw wrinkled clothes into the dryer with a wet washcloth. But I saved the ironing board, removing it from the cabinet, tucking it up in the rafters of the garage. My father ran the telephone wires where the ironing board had been.

For once, the TV isn't on. My mother enjoys the TV as background noise but to me, TV on in the daytime would be evidence that my life is over, reduced to watching other people live theirs. Pathetic talk shows hosted by interrogating men wearing bad ties. Saccharine game shows with bouncing blonde contestants winning trips to Bora Bora. So, go on, dude, tell us all about your new awful movie where you blow up planets in space. So, come on babe, lay all your cash on the table. Bet it all. Go for the win.

Somehow, I'm gripping a chipped mug of tea. It's cold. A circle of creamy film floats on the top. Sun bounces off a crystallized layer of fresh snow. Last night was a microburst. Huge flat potato flakes cover the spotty grass. It looked safe outside. It also looked silent, even better. How I wanted to sink into it. Be covered in silence, one bit at a time.

I want the house to myself. I want to take care of myself by myself. I want to take care of my children by myself. Instead of dropping like a stone in the morning, I want to slide out of bed as if I am made of gossamer. Dance down to the living room, roll up the rug, and slide across the oak floor in fuzzy socks. To let lightness take me over the way it used to. I don't remember what it is like to wake up and think that anything is possible. I wake up thinking nothing. When your internal light is on, people know. They're drawn to you, like moths. You look very bright today, they say. They used to say.

My head is heavy and my shoulders rise up as if to catch it. The sun beams in and cuts across the floor to where I sit on the loveseat, facing the backyard. Behind me is an expanse covered with a braided rug, the swinging cradle, and the radiator pinging heat. Above it, a pair of windows face the street. The twins are in the cradle wearing footie pajamas, a head on each end like a double ended pencil.

Outside, the shed appears as a sparkling snow-encrusted mound. Immediately upon moving in, I planned to transform the woodshed into a summer drawing studio. With a pencil or charcoal between my fingers, I was never afraid. I loved the anticipation in my body, how it travelled from the space between my shoulder blades and dove downward, gathering in my wrist while I selected the correct version of charcoal. I prefer vine charcoal. Its delicate curve a Victorian presentation of femininity—fragile, melancholy. Using it, I turned fragility on its head.

Enter the female model. Watch as she arranges her arms in the air like a statue from antiquity. She is demure, slender, but soft in her thighs and stomach. Her breasts are a C-cup. Her hair is long and her facial features are fine. Her hands and feet have prominent tendons. You cock your head to the left. To the right. Address your newsprint. The vine charcoal is a whisp in your hand. An invitation. Medium to paper, you disappear into a world of your own making. Shoulder becomes elbow becomes knee becomes ear—nostril. Vine charcoal is sooty. It crumbles in contact with the paper if you press too hard. You know exactly what you are doing. Afterward, standing back from the easel, your left arm across your waist, knuckles as a brace for your elbow, you congratulate your achievement. Your right hand holds the charcoal like a cigarette, palm open to the ceiling.

The male model is an asshole. Certainly, he's only here to irritate every young woman in the class. Every time you set up your easel, every week a different spot in the circle of student artists, he enters the room, unties his too-short colorless terrycloth bathrobe and sits facing you. Full fucking frontal.

What you wouldn't give for a view of his hairy back, his flat ass. But no. It's the same pose each time. His right foot on the top rung of the stool, his left foot on the floor. His right arm cocked, hand resting with his fingers toward the inside of his thigh. Elbow out. He takes up all the air.

You have few choices. Focus on his face—that fantastic hawk nose, caterpillar brows, and cleft chin—or his dick, at ease between his hairy thighs. You don't glance at the other girls. There's an unspoken covenant to behave like the boys and get to work. Focus. Think of negative space. Think of the man not as a man, but as an imprint. Take up your compressed charcoal, which is hefty like a railroad pin. Apply a flat razor to it and plane the ends to the point of desirability. Compressed charcoal is muscular. But with a little encouragement, you can coax it to lightness by smearing with your fingers, lifting darkness with a gum eraser. Fixative spray to contain the mess.

If only it worked. No matter how much fixative, a shadow appears on the opposite page when you close the pad. A twin. The drawings you made of the man are good. The drawings you made of the woman are boring.

We've lived here four years and I still haven't turned the shed into a summer drawing studio. My paints, architecture and figure drawings from college—all organized in their box and portfolio—are in the basement. I feel their exhaustion.

There is only time to feed the babies, clothe the babies, and change the babies. Only time for remembering to order heating oil before we run out—again—and to abandon my first shower in four days with soap in my hair because someone is crying and try and fail to not see my swollen body in the mirror as I throw back the curtain. There is only time to not brush Trevor's teeth properly.

Trevor is a drip down the back of my throat. The type of relationship Trevor and I had before was mother and child. Not ill mother of three, healthy mother of one. His delivery date of April 13th evaporated when I went into labor on April Fool's Day.

My first born, in a long line of first-borns: me, both my parents, both of my grandmothers, and two of my great-grandmothers. First born children are the practice children. I'm supposed to know what I'm doing by now.

Our early days together evolved from 5 AM. His wail a wail to trump all wails. My hands sliding beneath his warm vibrating body, lifting his small head to the nook between my shoulder and collarbone, his mouth snuffling and sucking at my neck.

Greg and I were renters then. Mrs. Mulligan beneath us could hear everything—including bad moods. I'd hustle to the kitchen. After feeding Trevor his bottle, I'd place him in bed with Greg, still asleep, and wait a moment before I took a shower. Greg's chest rising and falling. One arm under his pillow, the other tucked around our baby whose soft cheek provided his own pillow.

What's his name an elderly lady asked me at Kmart. Her jowls were lined with wrinkles and caked with foundation. She opened her patent leather purse and shut it; two gleaming brass balls snapped the artifact closed. She held a lace-edged handkerchief, the kind my great-grandmother used to keep between her breasts. *Look at these cantaloupes* she'd say, hefting them, deep in the throes of dementia. The handkerchief made its way toward my baby's face. She wiped up a stream of spit-up from his chin.

You know what they say? When so many boys are being born? There's going to be a war.

I could have said, *thank you. What a delightful old lady you are.* I could have said, *yes, my husband and I are making fortifications.* I could have pushed the stroller right over her, ditching her anti-blessing—akin to a curse—over the head of a peach-fuzz baby who smelled like lavender and milk. The fertilized smell. Instead, I smiled like an idiot and casually moved through the checkout line.

I have spent the last four years brushing his teeth, reading *Goodnight Moon* so many times his bedsheets could have recited it and stocking up on Goldfish crackers. Outside, several feet of snow wait for Trevor to make forts.

"Today," I'd promised him this morning. "Today you can play in the snow after pre-school. Grandma will be here." He was thrilled.

"Grandma can hold the babies so you can be with me, right?"

"Hmmm," I said.

"Remember when it was just us?" he said.

Just like that, a healthy part of me became diseased, cut loose, and floated away.

With the capacity for spatial relationships that he put to use with Legos, he used it to straighten me out like a four-year-old architect. It wasn't only that he recognized the spatial problem of not enough hands—he knew I hadn't thought of it. At all.

Where I used to have two free arms, now I have none. On the rare occasion they are free, I stare at them like they are exotic. I am not holding Trevor enough. This is the despair I sit with. Am heavy with. But I am also heavy with the house. Of its circular responsibilities. The washer, the dryer, the dishwasher—all have underlying demands. And the checkbook. I haven't looked at that in weeks. The cable is probably about to be shut off. Receipts for gas, groceries, and formula are likely crumpled, forgotten in Greg's coat pockets. No one tells you to remember to pay the electric company when the unexpected happens. They just expect that you can handle it. No one has asked me if I can.

My mother is still on the phone. I know without seeing her that she is standing in her favorite spot, the narrow space between my stove and sink. Her elbows rest on the counter. One leg slightly bent, one leg straight. I stand this way too.

Her spiral calendar is splayed open in front of her, a blue Bic in her freckled fingers. I know she is speaking with a close friend—Donna, or Diane, or Mary-Ellen. My mother has a different laugh with each of them. Her voice is breezy and I close my eyes again. The sun, the hum of appliances, my mother's muffled voice, soothes me back to sleep. Until her voice ticks up.

"She's doing just great! Yes! Tomorrow we've got the surgeon and we had some scans. No—no results yet."

I can't hear anymore because now she whispers. My head stretches out of my shoulders. I feel all my limbs. Something that had been dormant inside me crawls out of my skin and paces the floor. I hear the phone put back in its cradle. My mother enters the living room.

"Who were you talking to?"

I am casual. My mother doesn't notice the animal.

"Just Donna."

Everything about me goes dark. I spread the darkness. The animal bares her teeth.

"You know what's happening isn't happening to you, right?"

She is colorless. I don't care. My animal circles her legs.

"Not you. Me. So stop saying *we*. If you have to talk to your friends, don't do it here. Do it at your house."

I return my attention to the snow. I haven't left the sofa, but I've crossed the line.

My animal jumps onto the sofa cushion next to mine and cleans its claws.

My mother moves until she is standing in front of me. She's not sorry. She has that determined look. The look that she earned moving from Connecticut to Virginia—where she knew no one—following my father's whim. She worked two jobs to keep us there—parenting alone—while my father drove a tractor trailer cross-country leaving us over and over and over. Seven years later, she followed him back to Connecticut, even though she'd fallen in love with The South. In Connecticut, she started over. Again. In front of me, she wears the look developed from saving her own marriage. She's wearing her don't fuck with me look.

One hip drops and she shimmies her upper body. Her head bobs. One eyebrow is up.

Wanna rumble? She wears a fleece mock turtleneck with appliqued snowflakes. If I laugh it will be mania. This is not the time for mania. I've gotten a glimpse at the anger inside me and I like it. Even more, I recognize it. A nightmare I can enjoy. The repeating nightmare from my pregnancy—the panther woman pacing in front of my house—she isn't the woman Greg had his affair with. The panther is me.

SEVENTEEN

We are in the elevator. We is me, my mother, and the twins. We're travelling to the fourth floor of a medical building for a post-op appointment with Dr. Johns. This is the surgeon who removed the fluid from the lump in my breast. The one who called Dr. Robb to tell him his pregnant patient had cancer. This is the surgeon who removed the lump. It's been two weeks. A lifetime.

My mother said she could watch the babies on her own, but I suggested we all go. We all could use some air, I'd said, meaning me. My mother didn't bring up yesterday. I didn't either. We were polite, giving my animal space.

The elevator door stops at the second floor and two women get on. They notice my mother and me each hold a sleeping infant in matching everything—seats, blankets, the gold-plated hooded sweater buntings from Newport. One of the women turns to me.

"Twins?"

Duh, I want to say.

"Yes."

"Are they both yours?"

My animal is hungry.

My mother steps in. "They are both hers, but—"

The elevator stops at our floor. My mother follows me out. I turn to her once the door closes. "What exactly were you going to say? 'They are both hers, but—' what?"

My mother is sheepish.

"Nothing. I was just going to say that you couldn't carry both babies to term, so they did an operation and I carried one of them." She stares down the hall.

My mother, a woman who cannot ever tell a joke without laughing through the whole thing—nine times out of ten forgetting the punchline—and can't lie, just attempted to do all three. We look at each other. Our lips form mirrored Os. We bend at our waists, placing the baby carriers on the floor to hold our stomachs. We are silent until we stand up.

Frantic, glowing bubbles of hysterical laughter explode out of us. We lift the babies and continue down the hall. Bubbles bounce off the walls, slide underneath doors, into utility closets and physician waiting rooms—bursting.

I'm still smiling when we are shown into the exam room. I remain smiling even as I remove my top and a sports bra designed for Amazons. All that bottled up tension released, I recline on the exam table, propped up on my elbows like I'm sunbathing by an inground pool.

My mother sits inches from my elbow in a boxy armchair, the babies, by some miracle still asleep, at her feet.

Dr. Johns raps on the door and enters. This time, I really look at him, not just his neon sneakers. He's narrow in the shoulders and medium build. Sandy hair. Vaguely resembles the English actor Martin Freeman.

"How are we doing?" he says, washing his hands. He dries them and smiles at my mother.

"Good," I respond, surprising myself.

"Fine. Fine. Let's take a look," he says, still smiling, peeling back my johnnie coat.

He stops smiling. "Oh. Wow." His eyes are wide. I look down at my gargantuan right breast. He removes the adhesive pad covering the incision site. The incision is bright red, but I don't see any evidence of infection. It looks like it's healing. What I need right now is a nod. A smile. An application of a new bandage, a handshake, and a follow-up appointment in never.

Instead, he says, "The cavity has filled with milk."

My brain is processing—making incongruous connections. Trevor could have a cavity. When was the last time I took him to the dentist?

"What cavity?" I say, squinting at him.

"The cavity created when the tumor was removed."

"This one is drying up," I say, pointing to my left breast.

He looks at me hard. "The milk has to come out."

"What?" I say. But he's already at the sink with his back to me.

He turns around with a large gauge needle in his hand. It's as wide as a straw. The needle is connected to a cylindrical syringe, like large animal vets use to inject tranquilizer.

"Lie down."

I lie down. I turn my head toward my mother. Her eyes are wide. She breaks contact and concerns herself with readjusting the babies' perfectly adjusted blankets. I turn my face back to the ceiling hoping for a view of Yosemite. But Dr. Johns blocks the view with his head. I watch the needle he holds enter my skin. Feel the drawing up of the plunger. The syringe fills with what looks like Strawberry Quik. He removes the needle, turns to the sink, and squirts the blood-tinged milk down the drain.

"It's too bad you aren't nursing," he says, doing the procedure again. "You could have fed all the infants in the maternity ward."

Who was it who told me I couldn't nurse? Someone did. When I was discharged from the hospital, I remember handing my mother the weird looking, but expensive twin nursing pillow I was gifted. She returned it for cash.

I never wanted breasts. I never wanted a bra. I never wanted to say bra. The only reason for breasts was to feed babies and ballerinas didn't have babies, as far as I knew. They definitely didn't have breasts. Ballerinas had long legs and necks and prominent ribs. They might be grownups, but they looked like girls.

As a small child, I didn't notice any distinction between boys and girls. In the summer, I rode my bike and played outdoors without my shirt on. Shirtless was how my father mowed the grass and how the boys at the end of the street played basketball. When they stretched their arms to throw a basketball into the net, they jumped—inhaling—revealing ribs and shoulder blades. I saw their actions through their skin.

I had ribs. I had shoulder blades. Running bare-chested was a request for the air to touch me. Climbing our pear tree, I'd lie face first on a thick branch, its pliable bark meeting mine, and dangle my arms on either side, a backyard Bagheera in *The Jungle Book*. I imagined myself invisible in a white jungle. I was the whitest in a white neighborhood. If fair-skinned is on a spectrum, then I was almost all the way to the end. A cabbage moth. Light brown hair cut in a pixie; I'd fly out of the house. Up and down Diana Lane playing Zoo. Until it was time to play Wedding. When the neighborhood kids said I had to marry Bobby.

Bobby Johanssen was a few months older than me and lived across the street. Our mothers were good friends. Mrs. Johanssen was always cleaning something. Once, she was cleaning behind her oven and found a dead mouse. She got a new oven. After my mother visited with Mrs. Johanssen, my mother always told my father, "I could have eaten the cake she served off the floor."

One rainy day, my mother brought me with her to Mrs. Johanssen's. Bobby took me to his room. He shut the door and produced a stethoscope. I knew that game. To play Doctor's Visit, the patient had to lie down on the front steps of the doctor's house—the kid playing doctor—and be told what sickness they had. Strep throat was the best. You'd get a lollipop. Because it was pouring, I lay down on Bobby's bed. His stethoscope wasn't a toy like the one I had at home with a blunted syringe and play thermometer. It was a real one.

I had on my favorite sleeveless shirt. A ribbon ran through the neckline. I'd tied it over and over to get the loops even. The fabric was drawn together producing an oval keyhole. My skin visible.

Bobby stood over me. He was supposed to place the stethoscope on my belly, on top of my shirt. That was the way the whole street played the game. He lifted my shirt. I figured he was going to listen to my belly button where my baby was. I believed every girl had a baby in their body. It grew as she grew until she got married and the baby grew really big and had to come out. When I got bored feeding Baby Alive, I took the bottle of magic disappearing milk and pressed the hard plastic faux nipple inside my belly button.

Bobby bypassed my belly button for my heart. He pressed the cold round metal on my skin and I breathed in and out like at the real doctor's office. I sat up, ready for my turn and pulled my shirt back down. I held my hand out for the stethoscope, but Bobby didn't give it to me. He jumped up and down.

"I saw your boobies! I saw your boobies! Boooobbbbiiiies!"

I didn't know what boobies were. He pointed to my chest. "B O O B I E S!"

Whatever boobies were they sounded a lot like *Bobby's*.

I ran out of his room and down the hall to the kitchen, ready to throw Bobby under the bus. But I made the unexpected connection of girl to woman. I looked from my mother to Mrs. Johanssen. They both had what my mother told me was a *chest*. If I told Mrs. Johannsen that Bobby was the one to inform me that the correct term was *boobies*, Bobby would tell the whole neighborhood that I was a moron. Also, Mrs. Johannsen served real Kool-Aid, not prune juice like my mother. The Johanssen's had giant Fourth of July picnics where all the kids played with sparklers and ate as much watermelon and brownies as they wanted. I said nothing.

The next time my mother went to Mrs. Johanssen's and I had to go, I sat under the kitchen table while they visited. When the holiday picnic came and all the older girls stuck watermelon seeds on their foreheads, naming them after the boys they liked, I named every seed Elvis. A shy boy in my class with dark hair that fell into his eyes and beautiful dark eyelashes like the soon to be dead singer.

Our neighborhood was in the hills of Beacon Falls, a valley town up old route eight and over the Naugatuck River. I memorized the route in case I needed it. A right turn between the empty shoe factory buildings, past my school, uphill past the old house where no one mowed the grass, right turn at the house with the cement swan full of red geraniums, and a left at the vacant lot where we played spy in summer and sled down the hill in winter. Directly across from the house that we all saw a man enter carrying a pistol. Diana Lane was a dead end. Cul-de-Sacs were for rich people.

Before my sister was born, my mother had worked for Better Packages, a company that made water-activated tape dispensers. My father was a cable splicer for Bell System, eventually becoming American Telephone and Telegraph Company—AT&T. While he was training for his repairman test, he climbed the telephone pole across the street from our house. He wore spiked boots and a wide leather belt. The belt was around his waist and the pole. I watched from the window. When he got to the top, he removed his hard hat and waved it in the air. He also served in the state police as an auxiliary. The gray Stetson that was part of his uniform was kept on the top shelf in my bedroom closet.

Both my parents told me that bad men might try to take me. I should never ride my bike to the end of the street. I should stop at the empty lot and turn around. My greatest desire was to ride to the end of the street and keep going, to coast like the big kids did, down Cook Hill Road with my hands off the handlebars. I devised a plan. Inside one of the empty Sucrets tins my mother gave me, I hid a note for any bad man who spoke to me—and tried to take me. What they would want me for I didn't know, but I was pretty sure there would be chores.

A group of us were hanging out on our bikes by the vacant lot. A massive car slid up alongside. A man with a mustache rested his hairy arm out the window. "Hey, kids. Where does Cookie live?"

Cookie lived at the intersection of Diana Lane and Cook Hill Road in a derelict farmhouse. Cookie was a cook. He and Mrs. Cookie had older kids who ran wild. At Halloween, Cookie pretended to be a stuffed scarecrow slumped by the door. When you went to push the bell, he grabbed your arm. If you didn't scream, you got a 100 Grand Bar.

I eyed the man in the car. How could anyone tell if he was bad or not? I felt the pocket of my shorts. My tin with the note was at home on my desk.

The next time, I was ready. It was early. I was out on my bike for surveillance before the neighborhood woke up. I inched my bike past the vacant lot, pedaling standing up, all the way to the intersection. I was ready to go down the hill. I was ready for the guy in the station wagon to ask me—a pale girl on a black and white bike with a banana seat and monkey handlebars with plastic red, white, and blue streamers—if I would like to go to his house and wash his kitchen floor where there was a steady supply of Razzles and Almond Joys.

When the driver of the station wagon saw me, arms folded across my chest, straddling my bike, he stopped. He reached across the passenger window and rolled it down.

"Hey kid, where's Burton Road?"

He wore a white T-shirt, long sideburns, and thick glasses.

I reached into my pocket and threw the Sucrets tin in his window. Then I rode my bike home as fast as I could, skidding to a stop in the sand at the bottom of the driveway. Then I ran into the house, taking sanctuary by the washing machine and my father's work shirts hanging up. Inside the Sucrets tin was a ripped piece of wide-lined paper. I'd written I LIVE AT on one side. YOU SMELL on the other in multi-colored crayon letters.

When I turned eleven I wore a stretchy lace training bra twenty-ty-four hours a day. I didn't want boobies. I damn sure didn't want what my mother called them—*breasts*. Breasts were huge boobies. In the seventh grade, the boys in my class became fascinated by bras. They'd walk behind a girl on the way to the cafeteria and using a thumb and forefinger, snap her bra. Right at the catch, where it stung. The boys didn't do this to me. They did this to the girls wearing velour Gloria Vanderbilt jeans and feathered hair. I watched the boys' faces when the girls whipped around to smack them. The boys looked shocked that something they did got a girl to touch them—even if it was a slap. Breasts changed everything.

I hung back to be last in line on the walk to the cafeteria. No boy would dare snap my bra. By thirteen, I decided that if growing up was required, then I would become alluring. Beautiful, but mysterious, like Golden Age movie stars. Or Cybill Shepherd. A woman who was called alluring meant she didn't need a man. You could tell just by looking at her.

I have never been called alluring. I have been called stubborn.

EIGHTEEN

Greg can sit, motionless, in the overly warm exam room in the oncology wing, but I cannot. Waiting—such a colossal waste of time. Pacing—not as good as running, but close enough. Security professional that he is, Greg keeps his eyes glued to the closed door. I am a vibrating cocktail of nerves, skyrocketing estrogen, sleep deprivation, and nausea. Reaching up to touch my hair, I realize one side is matted to my head, the other side springs out. Evidence that a baby powder shower can only do so much.

My feet fit back into normal shoes, but I'm wearing elastic waist pants. Wearing pants that had been on sale next to a crate of avocados is bad enough, but I topped the ensemble with a pre-pregnancy spandex T-shirt. My breasts are heavy, the right one especially large—again. The new bandage covering the cavity feels spring-loaded. My skin is tender, but what lies beneath is not. It pushes and seeks an exit. God, my body is so stupid. The babies are on formula. My breasts should have eyes instead of nipples.

Now I've done it. I've thought about nipples. My eyes dart to the little doctor's sink and I wonder if I can express some milk on the left side—the only side possible—before the doctor walks in. I catch my reflection in the stainless-steel paper towel dispenser. My face and neck are the color of a ripe radish.

Briskly, the doctor comes in. Salt and pepper hair, early fifties. Wingtips with tassels. Even so, I can tell he's no mere runner. He's a marathoner. He looks like someone famous, but I can't think who.

"Nice to see you," he says, shutting the door. He's addressing Greg. "I'm Dr. Bee. Congratulations!"

What the fresh hell.

"Twins, right?" he continues, focused on Greg, who does not have a uterus or cancer.

"Yes, twins," I say. Dr. Bee walks over to Greg and shakes his hand.

"The results, what are the results—" I'm shifting from foot to foot as if trying to soothe my infants, who are at home with my mother and an aunt—although I couldn't say which one. My ears recoil at the sound of my own voice, overly sensitive from colic in stereo.

Dr. Bee retracts his hand. "Results?"

"The bone scan, the brain scan, the heart scan, the body scan, all the scans." I'm leaning forward now. I could probably take this guy.

"No one gave you the results?"

I have three options: express the milk, throw up, or faint. Fainting might be nice because then I would be unconscious.

"I'll be right back," he says, and disappears.

Ten minutes earlier I'd had sympathetic looks in the waiting room amidst the potted plants and pale wood furniture. Despite its quiet color palette of aqua and ivory, the waiting room was tight with restrained emotion and an unwashed, ammonia-tinged smell that hovered like persistent fog. The other patients were elderly. They used walkers, some used canes. None of them had given birth ten days before, four floors up in the maternity ward. How much time did they have left? Someone should be ushering them into a room. Someone should be gathering up their frail bodies in strong arms and telling them it would be all right. It couldn't be me. I wasn't there. I was in a well, using my own arms to help keep me afloat.

I stare at the door where the answers are supposed to come from. Dr. Bee isn't returning fast enough. I fall into Greg, burying my face in his shirt.

"What's wrong?' Dr. Bee says. I want to say *you*, but then I think how I dumped half the bottle of barium down the drain. He's going to tell me I need to take the test again. And I know that I won't. I'd rather have all my toenails removed.

Greg is rubbing my back. "We were ready to hear whether the cancer spread, but the waiting—it's too much."

I turn around and look at Dr. Bee. He has a folder with my future in it.

"Oh! Sorry about that," he says and opens my folder.

"I think I can help you. You'll need chemotherapy and radiation and—"

I don't hear what else he says because I'm under water.

"Dr. Bee," I say, bubbles coming out of my mouth, "Is there cancer all through my body?"

"No," he says, smiling like an advertisement for an orthodontist. "We got it all."

Richard Gere.

Dr. Bee looks just like Richard Gere in *Runaway Bride*. My left breast explodes. I'm a milk flood.

NINETEEN

Dr. Bee and Dr. Johns have had a meeting. I wasn't invited. I didn't even know about it until afterwards. At the end of their meeting about my body they decide they will cut open my right armpit and take out a few lymph nodes. Lymph nodes look like kidney beans.

When I tell Dr. Bee in his office that my sister used to hide her peas under the refrigerator and I hid my kidney beans in my armpit, he laughs, but my distract and flee attempt does not work. They are the screening mechanism for the body he says from behind his desk. We'll know for sure that no cancer cells escaped Dr. Johns says on speakerphone. Because I had two hours of sleep in a row I can say something intelligent. Will my treatment be any different if there is a positive kidney bean?

Silence. Greg has wisely said nothing, but I see the look Dr. Bee shoots him. I stand with my arms crossed like the sentry of my body. I know, I say, without a shred of doubt, that only healthy cells inhabit my body. But men like proof. Intuition means nothing. I wither under scrutiny. How can I *know* know? I have the surgery.

While I wait for the results, I walk around with a curling plastic straw popped into my armpit that drains fluid into a bag. I am not supposed to hold my children. I watch other people do it and settle for kissing them on their foreheads, the loving secrets I want to whisper to them remaining in my mouth.

The first night I take the Vicodin I've been prescribed. The second night too. Since getting off the migraine medication, Cafergot, several years earlier, I don't take pills. Not even vitamins. I eat vegetables instead. The third night, Greg gives me the side-eye when I lean forward on the sofa and dump another Vicodin in my palm. There's a one-and-a-half hour window between wailing, and I plan to live it up.

"Get me a glass of wine, would you?" I say to Greg, holding my magic pill up to the light like it's made of gold.

"Are you sure that's a good idea? Remember, Margie is coming over."

"All the more reason."

The doorbell rings and there's Margie in our living room wearing a new tracksuit. She sits in the rocking chair, "What can I do?" she says.

And I have a breakthrough. A Vicodin breakthrough. Gesturing with my empty wine glass, I point to a basket of clean baby clothes.

"Why don't you fold that laundry?"

Margie leaps into action, the nylon from her ass making a sound like tape being removed from the wood rocker. I sit back, unable to remember why I don't like asking for help.

The next day I wake up Vicodin free and tell everyone I'm doing it all myself. I hold my babies and my right arm blows up and becomes lymphcdcma. I tell no one. I wear long sleeves, even in bed. Dreaming the swelling away, I also dream myself a fantasy that I am normal, that I can't feel alone because I am constantly surrounded by people.

After seven days of watching lymphatic fluid drain into a plastic bag, my mother drives me to Dr. John's. With no warning, he pulls on the straw with a sharp tug. The part of the drain inside my armpit isn't an inch or two inches long as I had assumed. It's eight inches.

The results of the kidney bean operation are not in. I fill the space between not knowing and knowing by cleaning. I mop the walls, polish all the oak trim including around the doors and windows. Pouring vinegar into a steaming bucket of hot water, I sink to my hands and knees and soap the floor. The old-fashioned way. The only way to get to the corners, where calcifications of crumbs like to congregate.

When the phone finally rings, I am splayed up the basement stairs, toes on the landing by the back door, knees resting on one step, left hand holding me in a plank. My right hand is wrapped around a giant car washing sponge attacking the treads and risers. Take a good look at your staircase sometime. See evidence of a footprint and a high-water mark.

The news that my kidney beans are clean should be a celebration. I am past puckered. Fingers ribbed and flabby from hot water, eardrums ringing like the morning after I heard Def Leppard at the Merriweather Post Pavilion in Maryland. The inside of my left elbow is sore from dye injections and blood tests. Now this new scar is under my right armpit. No feeling there—the disembodied voice on the phone says—ever again. They say to be careful with razors.

TWENTY

I'm running in the woods, naked. It's dark. I fall onto branches that must have thorns because I'm full of holes. I get up and run harder. Thigh muscles strain, arms pump. I sprout sweat.

It doesn't matter. There they are.

If you have knives for hands and guillotines for mouths you don't need to run.

The moon is wide, red, and does not help me. When I collide with knotted roots and rocks, I slip, silent. I could stop, talk to the factory workers. Take my chances. I'm a blue-collar daughter.

The trees know better. They say *don't stop running. The flood is coming. They'll take your elbows, kneecaps, and heart and give them to others. Or eat them.*

I will be a trunk. Of no use. I outrun my breath and wake to the twins' cries.

Stupid trees. You can't outrun a flood.

TWENTY-ONE

Chemotherapy will likely push me into menopause.

"You know that, right?" Dr. Robb snaps his rubber glove. I am in his office for the post-partum check-up which includes off-hand reminders of my end of life-giving potential.

What does it mean, to know something? Did I hear it? Yes. I heard it. Delivered to me like a commonplace thing, like a deli sandwich wrapped in waxed paper. Do I ingest or absorb? I'm not hungry for any more casual announcements. Shouldn't there be a ceremony? Shouldn't I be wearing something other than a paper gown? Shouldn't my mother be here?

When I was ten my mother said, "You need to know something."

We were in her bathroom. She'd just finished smoothing my long hair with her brown Vidal Sassoon hairdryer. She picked up a vent brush and got busy even though there wasn't a single tangle. I knew what was coming. She was too late.

Last year, the daughter of her friend Mary-Ellen held my Ken and Barbie, he naked, and Sweet Sixteen Barbie in her pink dress with the white polka dots hiked up to her waist, to illustrate how babies were made. I was already halfway to knowing. Kimmie Pisarski showed me how to kiss the back of my hand and said that boys would try to French me and the best way to mimic that sensation was by sticking my tongue between my fingers. I'd begun to hold in my stomach to look thinner.

My mother put down the brush and lead me to her bed. We sat on the edge, both of us smelling like Breck. She held my hand and looked at the rug. My parents' closet door was open, and I could see the old pillowcase where my father kept his dismantled shotgun. My mother told me what I didn't know about boys and about my own body.

When the bleeding began, I was in the girls' bathroom at Seymour Middle School. I undid my camel-colored corduroys admiring the graffiti on the only stall with a door. Sitting on the toilet I observed a small bright red circle directly in the center of my yellow-flowered underwear. In the nurse's office, I said *I need a pad* like I was the captain of the period team. The nurse dipped her chin, smiled, and handed me what looked like a six-inch ironing board and felt like a stiff washcloth between my legs.

That afternoon I found my mother putting clothes into the dryer. She took me upstairs and gave me a skinnier pad and showed me how to wrap the used one—now with two red circles—with toilet paper and rest it neatly in the trash. At dinner my father choked on his hamburger when I told my mother that I wanted my own stash of skinny pads.

The next day was the sixth-grade class trip to Quassy. I walked around the small amusement park in ninety-degree heat with a thin panty liner between my legs. It didn't matter how short my denim shorts were, I was on fire. I went to the bathroom and added wads of toilet paper to the overflowing liner. Walking the park, I stared at women's asses, looking for an outline of thick padding. I went to the funhouse over and over, the wavy mirrors distorting my body past recognition.

Mary-Ellen was on the bandstand. Amazonian with a deluge of thick blonde curls, she sang, swinging the microphone back and forth like a jump rope. Her husband Jimmy played the drums. It never occurred to me to go backstage and wait for Mary-Ellen and ask her for another pad. The rest of my mother's best friends I called *aunt*. Their husbands I called *uncle*. Not these two. Their daughter called them Mary-Ellen and Jimmy too—Carole, my instructor of Barbie and Ken sex. Eight months older, Carole was perpetually directing me in backyard plays in the summer, living room versions in winter. Always large brown cardboard boxes I was supposed to jump out of. Or her little brother jumped out and I, wearing my mother's prom dress, meant to look frightened. I was a damsel in pink off the shoulder satin with a tulle underskirt and red, white, and blue Grasshopper sneakers.

One day, between acts, I noticed a Daddy Longlegs climbing the cement foundation of our house. "Don't kill it, don't kill it!" she said. It never occurred to me to kill it. Until now. I removed my shoe and slammed it on the spider.

"Now you've done it, you've ruined everything. Now it's going to rain," she said, throwing her hands in the air.

A small victory. When it rained that evening I smiled knowing Carole wouldn't want to come over anytime soon. When she finally did, she lay Barbie down in the bedroom of my dollhouse and lay Ken on top of her, grinding them together at the hips.

I leave Dr. Robb's office without informing him that I had had a meeting with myself, and we decided that there will be no chemotherapy. He hadn't believed me when I said there was something wrong with my breast, as if a woman couldn't have two conditions at the same time. If I had time, I would find a new gynecologist. I leave his chemotherapy + thirty-one-year-old = menopause comment on the checkup table like a cadaver.

This is what I do know: even without chemotherapy, I can't hold Spencer and Parker enough. I want to, but I need more arms. Or an extra pair of legs. Or something else, I don't know what. Maybe what I need is still on the shelf in Babies R Us, something no one else needs, like a Diaper Genie, but would save my life.

In the hour between Greg leaving for work and my mother arriving, I address my infants in a running silent monologue. They are at my feet, cuddled in pale blue fleece blankets, sound asleep in their car seats. I tell them I am not having chemotherapy. It will make me sick and obviously, I'm cured. The doctor took the tumor out for fucking crying out loud. I need to get on with the business of mothering.

I apologize for the mother they won in the lottery. I apologize for crying when they cry, but the pain has to go somewhere and why not the air that can hold it? I apologize for the night I passed their father on the stairs, me with one baby and him with the other, and he said, "I already fed him." I apologize for not knowing he'd already eaten and for referring to him as *one baby* and *the other baby*. I tell their closed eyelids *I'm sorry for not knowing which of you I held*.

I ask forgiveness for when we first came home from the hospital, how they cried, but wouldn't eat. The extended crying made me call the pediatrician's office at nine o-clock at night and the doctor prescribed chamomile tea. Which made Greg dash to the store, no shave, in pajama pants and his leather coat. How I had the kettle boiling when he returned, realizing as I poured the water over the teabag that I'd forgotten to ask whether the tea was for the babies or for me.

Reaching under their blankets, I touch their toes. All twenty of them. Magic in two pairs of baby socks. Their toenails are white and pink and as translucent as architectural vellum. There is a small part at the edge of a toenail where it meets skin, nothing touching the roundness but air. I kiss it. I say *a baby's heel is the beginning of adulthood, a sign of strength to come.* A heel is an example of something not yet needed, but already present, and required to support their journey.

I tell them I love them—telepathically—by holding their skin to my skin, my hands cupping their spongy heads, all the knowledge they will ever need inside. It's up to me to protect them. Wash them, cover their heads with hats and cradle their bodies in the crook of my arm while I play with their toes. The best I can do is have them side by side in my lap. Four wrinkly legs, four flailing arms, two tongues jutting out and in while my eyes move back and forth between their faces. I memorize the differences, subtle as they are. I place my face between theirs and whisper in their ears *I will always know you.* And I apologize for saying *fuck.*

TWENTY-TWO

Grocery List

I'm not having chemo. I'm not.

milk, napkins

TWENTY-THREE

My left breast is soft and milk-free. My right breast is another matter.

I'm back in Dr. Johns' office. This time, my mother and the twins are in the waiting room. Three syringe procedures later, while he has his back to me squirting Strawberry Quik into the sink, I lift my head off the papered table and look down on my breast.

Where my right breast had been full, and round is now concave. The outside part, near my armpit, is a complete structure, but the inside has collapsed, like a hole in the ground I once walked by in New York City, a high-rise razed, its basement exposed to the sky. I feel sick.

"Dr. Johns?" I can see the outline of the tumor cavity.

"Yes?" He stands over me, syringe pointed up, needle to the sky.

"My breast." I point to the space where it used to be. "Can this be fixed?"

Silence.

"I am a good surgeon."

"Yes, I know."

I have been assigned to reassure, probably at that meeting about my body with Dr. Bee that I didn't know about until after it happened.

"I don't want—" I say, waving to my crumpled self. "Will I look like this for the rest of my life?"

Dr. Johns lowers the needle, poised now a hair from my skin. Ready for one more extraction, the last few drops of pink maternal milk.

"You've got more important things to worry about," he says and plunges the needle in. This time, I feel it.

Afterward, he leaves the room and I sit up. I look down at my breasts. Pale and abused, they sag like they have been slapped. I'm pulling on the stretch cami with shelf bra built in when I stop. Carefully, I remove the newly applied gauze pad from my breast, wrap it in a paper towel and throw it in the trash.

At the reception desk, Dr. Johns' secretary, with whom my mother and I have regularly enjoyed chatting about celebrities, slides open the glass window.

"He wants you to come back in two weeks. Which would you rather, Dear, morning or afternoon?"

I lift both babies, a car seat in each hand and inhabit the steel-eyed look I've inherited from my mother, who recognizes it immediately and follows me to the door.

"Neither" I say, walking out.

My mother says, "Sorry!" to the receptionist.

I am many things. None of them is sorry.

TWENTY-FOUR

Other Things That Have Been Said

Hey, put on a shirt.
-Neighborhood Boys

I am four, playing in the front yard with Barbie and Evel Knievel. He is called an action figure because he has a stunt bike. Barbie owns a townhouse in the city, an A-Frame in the country, a collection of mint cars including an Austin-Healy, a sand buggy, an ATV, multiple campers, a beach bus, a boat, and a horse, but she is called a doll.

Kick him in the shins.

-My mother

When I tell her that a boy at the bus stop calls me *dog* every day.
I am eleven.

Where do you think you're going?

-the older brother of my friend Cathy from Girl Scouts

I am on the landing by their front door, about to exit and walk
home. He moves so close to me that the doorknob presses into
my back. He's tall but loose in his slightly flabby body. Menac-
ing in a khaki way. His shaggy dog sniffs my crotch. When he
moves the dog's snout his hand lingers. I lift my foot to kick him
in the shins but knee him in the balls. He doubles over and I
sprint home. My mother is proud that her Baltimore genes have
filtered down. I do not feel proud. I feel that language failed me.
I am twelve.

She has a nice shape.

-Grandma Eva to my mother

I am thirteen about to cannonball into a pool.

Heart Ass.

-Greg

I'm twenty-three, pulling on my jeans after having two orgasms.

Are you going to nurse your baby? Nursing is better, Your baby will be healthier.

-billboards, magazine articles, and the La Leche League recruiter who calls me unsolicited while the twins sleep to the white noise of the dishwasher.

Now that your breasts are smaller, do men still whistle when you pass construction sites?

-my father-in-law

I am washing lunch dishes in the sink of his house. I ignore him because that's how I have been societally trained to manage a raging asshole. Also, kicking him won't do a damn thing.

What do you mean you're not having chemotherapy? You can't be serious.

-my mother

Greg, did you know about this?

-my mother

Did you tell your doctors?

-my mother

The doctors said your recurrence rate is extremely high.
-my mother

Greg, reason with her.
-my mother

During this particular one-sided exchange, I methodically fold linen napkins edged with Battenberg lace, a wedding present, still steaming from the iron, as if I am planning a dinner party for Martha Stewart. I split like the slice on my thumb from doing too much laundry.

The first time I split was when Greg told me of his affair. The second time was when a single fertilized egg travelling my fallopian tube highway doubled itself. The third time is an ever-growing multiplicity: ChristineElizabethLasseKalafusWifeMotherDaughterInsurance-AgentInDanger

My cells keep splitting. I have two selves, then four, then sixteen. It's a habit. I cannot stop if I want to. I am currently 173,056 people.

TWENTY-FIVE

My mother is a megaphone. I relent to chemotherapy for peace, but also, what's one more surrender? I allow Dr. Bee to tell just one of the thousands of people I am the chemotherapy protocol. My mother writes the words down as he says them because she knows that whichever daughter she drove to this appointment is not listening.

I've been writing all the important things, the protocol of my life, since I was six when Aunt Barbara gave me a red bandana covered diary with a brass lock. The key was strung on red silk thread, a circle I wore on my wrist like a bracelet. At night in bed, I wrote my childhood prayers to God, lying on my back, index finger of my right hand practicing cursive in the air.

If that me recorded the chemotherapy drug names they would leach out of the paper, cover my hands, transferring to everything I touched. The mismatched pots and pans in the drawer of our oven, the twins' diaper bag, Trevor's toys. The Shaker-style four-poster bed Greg and I drove to New Hampshire to buy as newlyweds to save on shipping. The chemotherapy drug names needed to go from Dr. Bee's mouth to the cartoon bubble over my head, fed to a funnel in a black hole. To the place of negative space with all the other no-name words.

But when you surrender the ship, you get a close-up view of your captor. Before the pirate boards your vessel, pillage is an abstraction. Watching The Red Devil enter your vein undoes the ears. Adriamycin, Cytoxan, and Taxol are chemical poisons. They stop cell division, killing aggressive cancer cells like mine. The Red Devil also kills the cells for hair, fingernails, and short-term memory. I will have eight of these treatments, one every three weeks for six months. Then radiation.

Even though I have had successful surgery, even though the tissues around the tumor and lymph nodes are clear, the possibility of an errant triple-negative cancer cell in a thirty-one-year-old woman's body requires a full-on assault. The hider, the camouflage-er, that fucker of a cell, if given the chance, would unsheathe his blade and begin whacking away.

Chemotherapy is factory-made. How American. If I laugh now, I will give birth to a wrench.

The babies are at home with my mother and her team: Aunt Marti, Aunt Barbara, and my mother's sister, who I call Auntie, even though she's only eight years older than me. My mother doles out babies and tea. I drive myself to the hospital. Before the pirate comes, I must be tattooed. The nurse has large hands, but her head is massive. Giganta Nurse. No jewelry, no make-up, she doesn't need it. She has power. Needles and ink. She cleans her teeth with a four-star general.

"Come," she says. How can I disobey?

I navigated the familiar path to the hospital on my own, but now I am in the bowels of the hospital and don't remember how I got here. Swinging door after swinging door to blue gray metal passage with red tape on the floor labeled *no one admitted but personnel.*

Giganta Nurse acknowledges me with a twitch of her head, motioning to the table. There is no paper. The table resembles those in restaurant kitchens and morgues. I sit on the edge.

"I give you tattoos; you lie down."

What is that accent? Russian? German? Crazy?

Radiation tattoos are markings on the skin that make it easier for a technician to line up the X-ray beam which delivers focused photon radiation. Which will then cause mitotic catastrophe to any cancer cells that once inhabited the push-up bra area of my breast and is now a crater. That much I understand—at least, I hope to one day. Because no one explains to me what the tattoos will look like I imagine the kind in birthday party goody bags. Apply design to skin, cover with a damp paper towel, wait sixty seconds before peeling the paper away and there is a stegosaurus or a race car or Hello Kitty. Temporary.

Giganta Nurse approaches with a needle.

Somehow my shirt is gone, spit-up stained cami with the built-in bra is gone. I'm flat on the cold table.

Short needles require closeness. While Giganta Nurse's head is bent toward my chest, I inspect the white and black roots of her scraped back hair. Her scalp is flaking. Her nose is a hair from my right breast. I'm thinking *maybe she's far-sighted* when I notice the bottle of India ink, the same brand I use for drawing. She removes the cap of the bottle which does double duty as a dropper. Squeezing the dropper, a bead of watery blackness lands above the red scar. With the point of the needle, she slips the ink under my skin.

There are five more beads and five more pricks. The excess wiped with a white cloth. Then—an accident.

The last drop is a globule, right between the cavity of my right breast and the mound of my left. She jabs with the needle like she's in a hurry, and when the cloth comes away, the tattoo is not a dark blue dot but an island in my continental divide. Immediately I wonder what shade of liquid foundation will hide it. It cannot be mistaken for a freckle.

Giganta Nurse pulls away, noiseless shoes taking her to the sink where she washes her needle and caps her ink. I wait, wondering if I am done, if there is more. The water runs for a long time. I sit up and put on my shirt, stuffing the cami into my purse. When I leave, she doesn't turn around, the faucet is still on. At home, I take a shower and scrub my skin with nail polish remover, but the ink spots are still there.

The mind leaps backward and is satisfied. I once knew the magic my body could do. Headstands, cartwheels, one-handed walkovers, somersaults ending in a split. My favorite trick began as a handstand. Tipping, I'd bend my knees and cross them at the ankle, flying them apart at the last second, landing in a backbend. I like my legs, my teeth, pierced earlobes and not too slim hips. Hair like the Arc of the Covenant on my head. Breasts round and soft as molded ivory dust jelly. If you squeeze my breasts together now, you'll get a Rorschach test.

Once upon a time I was walking along, minding my own business. when someone took pen and ink and drew a cast-iron lid on the surface of the earth. The lid was left open, and I fell in. While I pretend that I can tread water forever, I know I can't. As weighty as I am, I can dissolve. My arms and legs paddle furiously—worthlessly. In the perfect sky circle created by the hole, a cluster of grocery coupons, late mortgage statements, and dryer sheets swirl slowly above my head like a kinetic sculpture.

TWENTY-SIX

"You were sitting there, writing something," Elizabeth says through the phone line. Elizabeth is another cancer patient. We are about the same age. She also has three children. Her youngest is four, like Trevor.

Yesterday, for the first chemotherapy infusion, I had been directed to a private room with a one-armed desk, like I'd sat at in high school, in the middle of the small room facing the door. All my surgeries had been on the right side of my body. My left side is an unplowed field. One of the veins inside my left elbow is the port to ferry the drugs. For this first chemotherapy, I dressed in a suit and heels because I read in *Cosmopolitan* you should dress for the job you want, not the job you have.

My nurse is an ageless ginger-haired beauty. Kathleen carried her supplies from patient to patient in a Bubbilicious-colored bathroom caddy. To distract myself from the bag of red liquid being hung from an intravenous pole, I set to addressing birth announcement envelopes. While preparatory saline and Benadryl drip in my left arm, I can write with my right hand. That was the idea anyway.

127

I'd chosen the twins' birth announcements from a specialty shop in Westville that went out of business a month later. Postcard-sized, the announcements are decorated with light blue and white stripes. Above each baby's name, weight, and time of birth, is a dime-sized watercolor illustration of a cherubic face. I try to use the back of my left forearm to keep the envelope in place. It slips and when I try to adjust it, I knock the entire pile of announcements to the floor. That's when I see Elizabeth, at the end of a line of doctors, nurses, and patients shuffling by. She is slight with a silk scarf wrapped around her head like Audrey Hepburn in *Charade*.

"I saw you too," I say, "your scarf was gorgeous."

"Who is your doctor?" Elizabeth asks. I tell her and she says that she will contact our oncologists to arrange all of our chemotherapy appointments to be on the same day and at the same time.

It doesn't occur to me to argue. It does not occur to the oncology receptionist either. Ten minutes after hanging up with Elizabeth, the oncology receptionist calls. Not only has the oncology receptionist volunteered my name and phone number to a complete stranger, but she has also rescheduled my second treatment.

When the oncology receptionist calls again, this time to remind me to come in to have my blood drawn in a few days, I want to ask if Elizabeth told her to.

I absorb the invasion. It feels like care.

I go by myself to have my blood drawn. White blood cell counts can dip, leaving a patient vulnerable to infection a healthy body can fight off. If the count is too low, the next chemotherapy treatment must be postponed so white blood cells can rebound. I do not know what *too low* means. I barely know what day it is.

After my blood draw I exit through the oncology hive to reach the tantalizing exit doors of what resembles a ferry terminal. What boat are you on—breast? Colon? How about Hodgkin's? There are counters with no signs. A series of mysteries. I'm looking for a support boat. I approach a woman sitting in a bank of three cubbies. The cubbies are awkwardly placed, as if the hospital had no place else to stash them. *How about here? When a first-class cabin becomes available, we'll let you know.*

A woman in a nurse's wrap coat, ID attached with a retractable cord, and a trio of thin gold necklaces around her neck smiles at me from her cubicle. "How can I help?" I smile back.

I'll take the Queen Elizabeth to Malta.

"Can you tell me about support groups?"

She rummages around her desk and pulls a bright yellow flyer out from between folders like a sleight of hand magician.

"This group meets once a month on Tuesdays at seven."

I look at the flyer. *Y Me.* Not a name I want to emulate.

"They're mostly elderly, but they're really nice."

"Do you have, um, any that meet during the day, maybe on the phone? Maybe, younger?"

"There's a teenage group that meets at Yale."

"I just had some babies—and I'm getting chemotherapy and I can't go out much."

I don't want pity, I want help. Pity means that death is likely.

She assesses me by quieting her busy hands.

"I'm not supposed to be doing this," she says.

Unfolding her hands, she rips a corner off a sheet of paper and jots something.

"Call this number," she says, handing it to me. "She had little kids when she had treatment. She even started a program here.

I haven't seen her in a while, but she's great—a great mountain of strength."

I could use a mountain of great.

Later that morning, I sit in my living room, full professional gear on, slip of paper in my palm. There is no name on it, just seven digits. The day is slipping away. If I don't call her now, before the twins wake for lunch, before my mother leaves her perch in the kitchen, before I have to run to the bathroom again to throw up, I never will. The number is a Hamden exchange. The mountain of strength could be right down the street. The numbers light up as I punch them with my thumb.

"Hello?"

"Hi! Hi. I hope this is OK, a woman at the hospital gave me your number."

"Oh?"

"Hi!" I say again, sucking in my breath like I can start over. The rest comes out in a single exhale. "I don't fit into any of the support groups I have twins and I'm doing chemo and she said you are great—a mountain—"

I'm a fucking idiot.

"Can you hold on just one moment?"

That's all I've been doing.

"Yes, of course!"

There's noise in the background on her end of the line. She must have placed her hand over the receiver because what I hear next is muffled. "Boys. Boys! I need you to leave this room now. Right now."

The hair on my arms stands up. I'm glad I still have hair on my arms.

"I'm so sorry. My sons and their friends just came in from playing basketball."

"How old are they?" I ask.

"They're in high school."

"That sounds amazing. I have infant twins and a four-year-old." I'm ready to have a light conversation—I want a light conversation because I am afraid of the dark. Maybe we can talk about celebrity pregnancies. About famous actresses naming their children after fruit and the state of Wyoming.

"Listen. I want you to listen to me." Her voice is hushed but tight. "There are some things I wish someone had told me. My boys were little—five, three and the baby just eighteen months—when I was diagnosed."

I'm pressing the speaker into my ear so hard the back of my earring digs into my neck.

"Cry," she says.

"What?"

This is not what I expected. On her end of the line I hear a door opening and closing.

"You have to cry. And laugh. And get angry."

She's whispering like these are government secrets. I picture her in a closet.

"You can't let the emotions stay inside. Don't hold it in. Do you understand?"

I'm nodding.

"Are you there?"

"Yes."

"Do you have help?"

"My mom." My voice catches.

"Perfect. Let her help. You need to get better."

I must have given her the wrong idea.

"I am better—I'm cured. The tumor didn't spread."

If I say it, maybe it will always be true. I want to show this woman I am a mountain of strength like her. Somewhere in my body is the strong part. Where is it?

"Yeah—well, I'm here to tell you that treatments are brutal, cured or not. And you aren't done. Not yet."

Then she asks about my treatment schedule and what drugs I'm being pumped full of.

I tell her and she sighs.

"Has your hair fallen out yet?"

"No. I had my first treatment last week—"

"Are you married?"

Barely.

"Yes."

"How is he?"

He's a good father. He's staying up all night with me. Neither of us is sleeping. He's repentant—I hope.

"He's supportive."

"Good. Does he have anyone to talk to?"

I want to tell her that I really don't give a shit.

"I don't know if he's talking to anyone besides me."

There's a loud crash. Teenagers laughing.

"I'm really sorry, but I have to go."

I wonder if the crash was a basketball sailing through a window and I want that problem instead. I imagine her kitchen, classically updated, heavy French doors, brass hardware. Always food in the refrigerator and an oil man that arrives without having to call. Her sons are handsome and casually confident without being arrogant— evidence of solid parenting. I want to sleep in her spare bedroom because a woman like her always has room for guests.

I'd tuck myself in under her eaves wallpapered with rose buds. I'd come downstairs every morning to the kind of family bustle only a guest considers charming. Her house would be a safe place to ask what happens after the false sense of security of treatment. How to be certain I won't die before my next birthday. If it's weird that I keep looking at my breasts. On a scale of awful what number am I for not bonding with my babies. Confess that when I drove home from the library two days ago I almost took the onramp to the highway. That I fantasized not looking back and crossing the border to Canada. How do I stay married? How do I cry, laugh, get angry and take care of infants, a preschooler, and alleviate the fears of my entire family? How do I live?

"Listen," she says. "Are you listening?"

I nod. "Yes."

"Good. You are going to be OK. Do you hear me?"

I can't say anything. Fat tears run down my face and my throat is paper.

"Are you there?"

"Yes," a whisper of tissue.

"You are going to make it."

A click. She's gone.

I walk to the kitchen and put the phone in its cradle on the wall and look at it. My mother opens the microwave and puts a mug of tea in it. "Who was that?" she says.

"I don't know," I say. As is expected in espionage, neither of us gave our names.

My white blood cell count is solid, so I can have chemotherapy number two. But Elizabeth's isn't. The oncology receptionist, a woman who is probably in the wrong job, tells me this on the phone.

When I show up the following week for my appointment with The Red Devil, the oncology terminal has been rearranged. The confusing counters are gone, replaced by one center desk. I want to thank the nurse in the cubicle, tell her how much it meant to me to speak with someone who successfully navigated treatment and raised her babies to men. That I will never forget her parting words.

An older woman with a confection of white hair sits behind the only desk. I ask about the nurse wearing the trio of gold necklaces.

"She sat there," I say, pointing to a potted palm. "In a cubicle. There were a bunch of cubicles."

"I'm sorry, Dear," she says, her soft blue eyes patient as if dealing with a small child. "I've been here for years. It's always looked like this."

TWENTY-SEVEN

It's five in the morning. The cast iron radiators are silent, the shades down. The darkness of the living room belies the intense activity on the sofa where I attempt to get two bottles into my babies' hungry mouths without dropping a bottle or a baby.

When I have the twins to myself, I pray to transform into the Hindu God Shiva Nataraja, the one with two sets of arms. Unlike Shiva, I don't have a serpent around my neck, the Ganga River flowing from my hair, or a trishula—similar to the Roman God Neptune's trident. My only tools are my body, even if shafts of hair release from my constantly tingling scalp, arms, and legs, stripping me bare.

Parker is in the crook of my left arm, supported by a pillow. My left hand, twisted at the wrist, holds his bottle. My feet are perched on the coffee table in mismatched slippers. Spencer rests on my thighs, his head near my knees, sucking down the contents of the bottle I hold with my right hand, elbow aloft. The hard part is over—lifting them out of their cribs, and down the stairs to the

135

kitchen, where I execute a mini backbend, one baby draped over each shoulder to retrieve the bottles, while they roar like lions.

The rule of numbers dictate that I cannot hold them the way I want to: one at a time, nuzzling their necks and touching the fine blonde hairs that grow past their hairlines. But if I move a millimeter, the nipple of Parker's bottle will pop out of his mouth, and I'd need my right hand, currently occupied.

Feeding twins is like real estate—location, location, location.

Greg, freshly showered and dressed for work, glides down the stairs. His suit jacket draped over his arm, he walks to each living room window, snapping up the shades.

"I've got a meeting and the weather isn't great, so I'm leaving now."

He leans in to kiss me, tie hanging perilously close to Spencer's bottle. I resist the urge to pull away. It doesn't work. He says nothing, instead he plants a kiss on each baby's forehead.

There's no time to ask him to put on the kettle, turn on the TV or burp the babies while I use the bathroom. The polished wing tips of his Florsheims glow as he walks through the kitchen, down the stairs, out the back door, to his car. The extra arms of a Hindu god are not sufficient. I need arms that have reach. I need *Mr. Tickle.*

Mr. Tickle is an illustrated character who is orange, round, wears a blue Derby hat, and has freakishly long bendy arms. In first grade, I read the book over and over wishing I had bendy arms. I imagined lying in bed, like Mr. Tickle, while my arms went down the hall. Instead of retrieving a biscuit, I retrieved Ballerina Barbie. Instead of walking to school and tickling the teacher through a window, my arms would stretch across my driveway, climb up my best friend Mari's house next door, and open her window. I'd make her bed, so her mother didn't get mad.

Mr. Tickle is a danger to the public. Mr. Tickle punks a police officer, a grocery clerk, a train conductor, a butcher, and a mail carrier—all depicted as men. Which is probably why the book is still available.

Greg's car starts, and a moment later, I watch him drive up the street, through the shadeless windows, as if he wanted to make sure I saw him drive away.

I don't need to touch everyone in town while hiding around the corner. I just need to touch one person. And away go my arms. Out the front door, across the lawn, and up the street to the stop sign where they grab hold of Greg's Toyota—yanking it down the hill and back into our driveway. My hands pull Greg out of the driver's side door and back into the house—his briefcase and wing tips landing in the snow. I hand him the babies and he hands me the keys and I drive to the airport where I board any plane that can ferry me to the tropics. Where the only assault on my body is the sun.

My arms are only human and so is the rest of me. I don't want to tickle Greg. I want to kick him in the balls. For his own protection, it's a good thing I am weighted to the sofa. I crane my neck and watch, through another snowfall, the taillights of the Toyota take my husband out of sight and out of reach. Crying in the dark is never a good way to begin the day. Besides, how would I get a tissue?

I'll never be a God, Hindu or otherwise, and the last time I looked in the mirror, I wasn't orange. I'm a woman who hasn't been trained for the job she has. The babies have fallen asleep, bottles empty, mouths wet with milk. Using the one ab I have left, I heave myself off the sofa, carefully moving the twins to the cradle by the window. They don't wake up. A shower transforms from fantasy to reality. Hot water pelts my back. I'm standing in two inches of tub water because my long hair clogs the drain. But the babies sleep. Twenty luxurious minutes. By attempting the impossible, sometimes I succeed. Even if I do it badly.

When I was young, I would lay my head in Grandma Rose's lap, her pale hands cupping the top of my head, like a blessing, then move slowly down, molding my hair to my neck and shoulders. For Trevor, my hair is a million silky blankets. When he made the move from crib to bed, he began wrapping his arms around my neck, entwining his fingers in the thickness of my hair at the back of my head, knotted together, both of us in his single bed, with our noses touching until he fell asleep. The loss of this essential comfort is a punishment doled out in strands. I prefer my lumps all at once.

I am inspired by the idea of a hair shaving party from a newscaster on CNN. She stops reading the latest reports from Afghanistan to say that cancer is on view everywhere, including TV. Which is news to me.

My experience is Victoria's Secret supermodels with perfect breasts selling bras and actresses shilling L'Oréal hair color telling me I'm worth it. Under the bright lights of the news station, the broadcaster says she invited her family to shave off her hair. Like it is an act of love. Then she reaches up to her head and takes off her wig on camera. I know that she does this for millions of people to see. To reduce stigma of illness, to show that a woman is still a woman whether or not she has hair or breasts. But I also know that she's staring at me.

I invite my parents and in-laws over and buy cold cuts and Kaiser rolls. My mother makes her thousand-calorie-a-bite macaroni and cheese. On the dining table are my sewing sheers and Greg's electric manscaping hair clippers. One chair is pulled away from the table and a stool placed behind it. The grandmothers stand, holding a baby each. Trevor stands on the stool. Greg stands behind Trevor.

My father holds our video camera, recording. I tell him where to stand and to make sure he gets a little of everyone in the scene, like I'm making a documentary for HBO.

When I called my hairdresser, she said shaving long hair would hurt. *It gets caught in the clippers* she said. She advised tying my hair up in little ponytails, then cutting below the rubber bands, then shaving. Before the grandparents arrived, I stood in front of the bathroom mirror, creating a hair sculpture. I sit down in the dining room chair. My hair resembles a multi-jet fountain.

When I was five, my favorite thing about myself were the ponytails on either side of my head. I loved the way the tips of my hair brushed my shoulders. I loved it when one of the older girls on the street braided my ponies at the bus stop and how when I boarded the bus, the driver, a usually gruff woman who smelled like gasoline said *Well don't you look like the Vermont Maid* after the famous illustration of a girl featured on bottles of maple syrup.

My mother's hairdresser was named Maurice. Maurice cut hair in the parlor of his big Victorian house in New Haven on Chapel Street. Sitting in front of a mirror that reached the ceiling, Barbicide cylinders beside it on a marble topped table like coffee percolators with aqua blue water cleaning tortoiseshell combs with teeth like whale's baleen, my legs sticking straight out from his large, crackled black leather swivel chair, he cut off my ponytails.

My eyes, nose, and mouth grew with each snip of his scissors, morphing from child to adult. Maurice, in his heavy black shoes, swept my long, light brown hair with a hint of curl into a fluffy pile and down a chute in the floor. *There*, he said to my mother, *you have a pixie.*

Greg doesn't make a move toward the scissors, so I hand them to him. He cuts off my ponytails. I hand him the clippers. My father zooms in on Trevor moving the clippers in a single pass across my head. Something is bubbling up. Before I can reign myself in, I laugh like when I was sixteen, cresting the eighty-five-foot climb in the front seat of Rebel Yell, a wooden roller coaster in Virginia, on a dare.

Trevor drops the clippers, and they buzz in a circle on the hardwood floor. When I pick them up, he jumps off the stool and hides under the dining room table. The grandmothers rock the babies back and forth. Greg makes passes on my head. My father zooms out. Trevor pulls off his socks. It's time for lunch. My father-in-law is already in the kitchen, stealing slices of ham.

The week before, my mother and I drove to Lucinda's. From the outside, the salon looks like any other. A large, legible sign and posters of hair models in the window. But the place has a side entrance. *It's for the men* Lucinda tells my mother and me. *Their egos are so fragile, especially the bald ones.*

She says this standing between Styrofoam mannequin heads wearing wigs. The wigs have categories: Budget, Posh, Luxury, and Celebrity. All synthetic. When I touch one, it feels like plastic. The scent is a cross between car oil and Neutrogena soap. My mother insists on a real hair wig. The price is one thousand dollars. I don't have one thousand dollars. Lucinda says *sometimes insurance pays—if it's a medical reason.* My mother whips out her credit card.

My new hair is originally from the Mediterranean. Long and blonde, like my original hair. Lucinda places it on my head and cuts me wispy bangs. She gives my mother a receipt and me a white plastic shopping bag with a Styrofoam head in it. When I get home, I open the doors of the linen closet and place the head with its hair inside.

Once the grandparents go home, the twins and Trevor are asleep, and Greg is in the bathroom, I retrieve my new hair, bring it to the bedroom, and place it on the dresser. I take off all my clothes and assess myself in the mirror. The skin on my head barely camouflages the skull beneath. Collar bones protrude. The left breast is round, full, with a quarter-sized areola and a pink pearl-button nipple. The right breast has a slash where the scalpel pushed in, continuing inward and upward toward the sternum. Full on the outside. Flat where cleavage should be.

A valley instead of a mountain.

TWENTY-EIGHT

In 1955, my father was nine years old living with his parents on Gardner's Lane in Ansonia, above the Naugatuck River, in the Lower Naugatuck Valley. My mother was eight years old living with her parents upriver, thirty-six miles away, on Sherman Street in Torrington, in the Upper Naugatuck Valley.

Living in a valley means forever going down and coming back up. Living in either the Lower or Upper Naugatuck Valley today means that to get anywhere, you are forever driving a maze of steep streets with names like *Crooked S*, or *Cliff*, or *Rockledge Loop*. You are forever passing factories—largely vacant. These buildings were where copper, brass, rubber, plastics, iron, sheet metal, textiles, foundry products, clocks and corsets were once made. Living in The Valley means forever traversing bridges over the Naugatuck and the Housatonic, rivers that generate hydroelectric power bringing light to your town, job, and your house.

But growing up in the Connecticut River Valley in the late 1950s and early 1960s meant never being far from the Great Flood. It meant walking or cycling your small legs past the rebuilding at

Ansonia Copper and Brass, Chromium Processing, Farrel-Birmingham, Housatonic Wire, and Sponge Rubber Products—skeletal evidence of a waterlogged week in August, 1955.

Hurricane Connie hit first on August thirteenth and fourteenth. Five days later came Hurricane Diane—the second and final nail in the coffin. Together, the twin hurricanes dropped over twenty-four inches of water. Dams failed and every bridge over the Naugatuck River was either damaged or destroyed. Over eight hundred homes were demolished and eighty-seven people died. A *Sunday-Herald* reporter wrote that the aftermath was *a staggering toll of death in a shroud of mud.*

My father remembers the Great Flood like this: no drinking water. He remembers driving with his father away from the Naugatuck River, up into the hills of Seymour, to the property of a wire company where there was a naturally occurring artesian well. Clean, safe water ran up a shallow pipe and spilled out over the grate. There was no stopper. My young father waited in line, filled his jugs, and climbed back into the car. They brought the good water home to Grandma Rose for drinking and for cooking.

He remembers watching an entire barn float down the Naugatuck River, slamming into a bridge, the barn splintering like brittle bones. He remembers Ansonia's Main Street under four feet of water. When the water receded, there was four feet of mud inside Farrel's, the factory where his father worked in the erector shop. When the water receded, my grandfather shoveled mud out of the factory directly into a train car, its original purpose had been to deliver recently forged parts to sugar mills in Chile. But the first thing my father remembers is his father taking him to see *The Gun That Won the West* at the Strand theater in Seymour between hurricanes. Water lapped at Route 8. My father held a red and white fishing bobber in his hands. He dropped it and it rolled under all the seats to the screen.

My mother remembers the Great Flood like this: no electricity. She remembers kerosene lamps in the living room at night and the sound of helicopters overhead. She remembers her parents' relief that somehow—magically—her father's bakery had been spared. Each of my grandfather's bread kneading, batter blending, and buttercream whipping mixers stood clean, dry, and ready for action.

She remembers that immediately after the raging waters receded, a man built a house on the empty lot next door. During the flood, he had escaped his house perilously close to the banks of the Naugatuck River by climbing out a window. His wife couldn't.

"My parents, nor anyone in the neighborhood ever called him by his name," my mother says. "We said, 'there goes the man who lost his wife in the flood.'"

This is the thing about experiencing floods: in the midst of them, you are cut off from news and outside help. This is the thing about experiencing trauma: in the midst of it, you feel cut off from news and outside help. Even if help is right there, wearing a fuzzy sweater and bearing packages of diapers. Even if it arrives at your house Monday through Friday from nine in the morning to five in the afternoon, ferrying whatever emergency reinforcements are necessary. Like bringing Kleenex. Like powdering babies' butts. Like feeding your babies in their car seats on the table while calling out to you from where you stand—stranded—in the living room wearing yesterday's clothes including a fleece ski hat holding a collection of mugs of once hot tea.

The messages coming from the mainland are reminders to return Dr. Robb's phone call, decide the date for the twins' christening, and plan Trevor's fifth birthday party. But you can't move because you're stuck in the mud, staring out the window, wig behind you, perched on the banister.

I don't have the safety of distance to assess my loss. I worry about surviving and when I am not worried about surviving, I worry about how not surviving will affect my children. I worry that I am not doing survival properly in this flood with no forecast of stopping. I close my eyes when I drive past graveyards—which seem to be sprouting up everywhere—a practice I would tell anyone else is a surefire way to end up in one. There is no way to ignore that I am drowning.

I never allow myself to say the word *death*.

TWENTY-NINE

I'm in the twins' room, leaning against the window jamb, freshly folded onesies tucked under my left arm. *Just what we need, another snowstorm.* I exhale onto the glass, as if a circle of warm breath can conjure spring. I turn my head toward the empty cribs. It's Saturday. Greg has taken all three children to his parents' house.

"And what are you doing, you lunatic? Laundry."

I flick the center of my forehead with a finger.

"Only crazy people talk to themselves, right?"

I cock an ear to the ceiling expecting an answer. Stranger things have happened. The house says nothing.

Pushing away from the window, I plop the onesies on the tall dresser I found last summer at a yard sale and painted. When I open the top drawer, a chip of Dove White flakes off. The chip lands on my bare foot. It's not sad. It's tragic—and evidence that everything I do is futile. "Fantastic," I say, slamming the drawer shut. It sticks on one side. I whack it with the bottom of my fist. It doesn't budge. There is no water in the well that should be filling

146

my eyes. Even so, something is bubbling up. Turning my back on the dresser, I face the storm.

The only thing between me and the storm are two panes of glass. Shoving the heels of my hands beneath the top rail of the window, it flies up. A large hook secures the storm window at the windowsill. Releasing the hook from its eye with my thumb, the storm window swings outward a few inches, like a book being opened. Like an invitation. The hook dangles like a key.

It's a long window, and a weird size. No ready-made shade would fit. I sewed its soft-fold roman shade. When I found the light blue and white striped cotton fabric in the remnant bin at the high-end store, it felt like a win. No one but me can raise the shade correctly. Greg or my mother did it last. The fabric is bunched up on one side, relaxed on the other. Bending at the waist, I seize the hook, pushing the storm window out further until my head is outside. Directly below my head, the cement patio is as soft as a down pillow.

Shielded from the snow, I lean out further, walking my feet to the wall until my toes bend at the baseboard, as if they could climb it by themselves. The storm window and I are horizontal, parallel partners. I'm affixed like Nannie Dee, the carved figurehead of a witch on the bow of the famous British clipper ship *Cutty-Sark*. Instead of a horse's tail in my hand, I have a hook.

I took so many romantic poetry classes in college, I received a minor in English Literature. I used to think it was a funny accident. It's not so funny now that Robert Burns' lines come to my head.

Coffins stood round like open presses,
That shaw'd the dead in their last dresses

The next thing in my head is the ghost story I heard from the older kids on the bus on the drive to Seymour Middle School, always around Halloween. After the waters receded from the Great Flood, coffins landed in the school's parking lot. The coffins—the kids pointed out the bus window as we travelled downhill—were from Trinity Cemetery next door to what had been a German Lutheran Church and where I took dance classes. The coffins had floated out of their graves, riding waves down West Street and took a right turn on Pine Street. Some of the coffins were missing their lids. Decayed bodies, the kids said, had been opened to the sky.

This snow-covered landscape is my ocean. I could fall into it and be covered, one white wave at a time. It's a seduction, the beauty of it. I close my eyes. The wind kicks up. I'm being pelted with bits of ice. I squeeze my eyes shut harder. The tops of my thighs dig into the sill. I release my grip on the hook—*you don't want to miss the lilacs.*

I open my eyes. The lilac buds are encased with ice like glass paperweights.

I see myself, half of me outside, half in, an impossible escape. Quickly, I lower my arm and walk backward into the nursery, bringing the hook home, gliding it into its partnering eye. Palms on the top rail of the double hung window, I hear the weight, hidden within the window casing, lift, when the window is closed again. My heart pounds.

Spinning away from the window, lurching to the hamper, I gather dirty footie pajamas, towels, and burp cloths. I bury my face, breathing in spilt formula, baby shit, and Lavender Aveeno Comfort Bath. I don't want to lift my head. I don't want to look out of the window. I don't want to bring down the roman shade and lift it up the right way, each thin ribbon travelling through the small plastic rings I hand-sewed on the lining. I force myself. I can't avoid windows for the rest of my life. The ice has stopped. It's snowing again. The flakes, flat and broad, float slowly to the ground like ash.

THIRTY

I can't breast feed, brush my hair, or avoid windows, but I can run.

I am not a fast runner. I am a plodder. Every leap of air is ruined by the impact of gravity. Things jiggle that I don't want to jiggle. My thighs and calves. The cheeks on my face. My other cheeks. So, really, I'm a fast walker who hops. Even if it's sloppy as hell, running gives me space. Running, I'm attached to nothing but the earth and even then, only one foot at a time.

As a child, I was fond of meandering. In the Seymour neighborhood we moved to when I was nine, I meandered in the woods across the street, observing tree roots and teaching myself to whistle through blades of grass. As a newlywed, I walked every morning before work at Maltby Lakes. Owned by the Regional Water Authority, the lakes were created as a reservoir in the 1800s. In the 1990s, the water was too full of chemicals. So, they opened the land up to the public, for a small fee. Pay it, and you receive the numerical code that unlocked the gate to miles of trails mostly in West Haven and Orange. The Evergreen Trail hooks into New Haven, skyscrapers just down the street.

One November I came around a bend where the trail curved up and around boulders. I raised my eyes from the path. Ten feet from my cheap slip-on sneakers was a stag. His huge sharp antlers were in direct contrast to his soft brown eyes. Snorting in reverse, he released two barrels of steam at me in the crisp morning air. Telling Greg later, I swore I smelled the stag's breath. The stag leaped into the air like he had springs for legs. I never heard him land.

It was on one of these walks, about a year after our wedding, that Greg said "Let's have a baby. My back is already sore, and I don't want to be an old dad." He was twenty-five. I didn't want to have a baby right away. I wanted to go to Europe. "Europe will still be there," he said.

After Trevor was born, my walks were only on weekends, Greg beside me wearing our baby in a pouch. Once we moved to the Witch House, I began walking at night. My walk was always the same. Down Dickerman, across Murlyn, up Home Place, down Evergreen, to Whitney Avenue, Sleeping Giant Drive, Kenwood, back to Evergreen and a left onto our street. The whole cultivated trek was a mile and a half of residences and whizzing cars. It was reliably brief and dull as an eraser.

I bought a bright yellow radio that strapped onto my upper arm with Velcro. The earbuds connected to an adjustable thin and shiny metal headband. One Saturday, when Trevor was two, I left him tucked under Greg's arm, both of them napping in our bed, adorned myself with the radio, and ran out the back door. I didn't run fast, but it wasn't dull. Listening to The Cranberries and Rage Against the Machine, I played games with myself. Could I make it to the far telephone pole before a song ended? Could I run uphill? Sometimes, I could do both.

When it rained, I jogged in the affordable gym up the street. Measuring my speed while my feet slapped against the treadmill belt, I'd look up from my low digital pace and admire young college bodies moving effortlessly between the weights downstairs then jealously watch them sprint upstairs to the loft, to the elliptical machines, to the stationary bikes—to the treadmill next to mine.

By the middle of April, after the fourth round of chemotherapy, I miss the gym. I romanticize how wonderful it will be to be surrounded, not by sick patients in the infusion room—where I am held captive every three weeks for four hours—who cannot stop whispering tales of cancer recurrence in my ear, but by healthy bodies happily ignoring me. I convince Greg that I'll be fine. "The gym is five minutes away. What could happen?" I say, as if falling down our stairs two weeks earlier had been a hallucination.

It was the middle of the night, but I hadn't tripped. I took the first two steps normally. At the third step, my legs gave way, like the German *wackelfigur* giraffe an elderly aunt allowed me play with as a child. The wooden toy was just a few inches high. I would press my thumb under the base and delight in the animal collapsing, limb by limb, until it was a jumble. Removing my thumb, the giraffe popped back to health. I hadn't been able to pop up. I was a jumble on the landing, a wailing Parker in my arms.

At my next white blood cell count, I accosted Dr. Bee, telling him I couldn't do anymore chemo unless he lowered the dose. It was only luck that our stairs had a landing and Parker and I didn't sail down the entire flight, cracking our heads on the cast-iron radiator at the bottom. Dr. Bee had looked back at his own diplomas on the wall and said *I do know what I'm doing.*

Isn't medication decided by height and weight I'd said, extending the waistband on my jeans to illustrate the forty pounds I'd rapidly lost. Dr. Bee called a nurse in to weigh me. He sat down on his rolling stool and pulled out his calculator like he was doing trigonometry. I was right. My dosage would be lowered. I was too angry to celebrate.

"Well, I'm going to the gym," I say to Greg's stoic expression. "Like it or not." Greg doesn't say a word. Our marriage might have a chance.

I arrive at the gym and holding onto the metal railing, slowly ascend the stairs to the loft. My father is in the far corner straddling a stationary bike.

"Oh, you go here?" he says when I approach him with my hands on my worn spandex covered hips.

"Greg called you."

"Who?" he says, looking at a spot over my head.

"You're the worst spy ever," I say spinning on my heel, marching to the treadmill no one wants, the one directly in front of the huge TV playing *Jeopardy!* with the sound off. Punching the pace arrow, I hit four, five, six, not fast enough, six and a half—now I'm sprinting. I haven't run in over a year, which means I'm also hyperventilating. I focus on the glass pendant lights illuminating naked steel beams of the flat roof. I run toward the lights, eyes narrow, panting. The lights meet me, and I run through them, light bulbs searing my insides—a cauterization that is a brick wall to dividing cancer cells. The only thing multiplying is my bad mood. It's a white-out.

Tomorrow I decide *I'm running outside.* I don't ask for permission. I wait to hear Greg's car door close in the driveway, a reverberation that comes through the kitchen wall, to the step under my ass, where I sit, bouncing a baby on each knee. Before he can put down his briefcase, before he is all the way through the back door, I place a baby in each of his arms. I am already running before the door shuts. I sprint for miles, never walking, because if I slow down, the monster will get me. The multi-headed monster that is cancer, infidelity, diplomas, and ridiculous people in grocery stores who ask, as I ease the twins' double stroller into the check-out line—when—if—how—I'm going to try for a girl. *Did you do fertility drugs? No* I want to respond, *I did LSD.* I sprint, an hour each night, buoyant.

I don't measure myself against a number on a treadmill, or the distance to the telephone pole. My legs beat like the drums of whatever rock song blasts in my ears. I don't see houses or cars. I extend my route, downhill, past the graveyard, toward the Sleeping Giant. I return home red-faced on endorphins and chemotherapy drugs that I hope are working and anti-nausea drugs that aren't.

I don't stop running at the back door. I take the kitchen stairs two at a time, wind through the kitchen, leaping over hurdles—baby gyms, clusters of Hot Wheels—grab the top of the square newel post and propel myself upstairs to the bathroom like a slingshot. I whip off my spandex top and pants before falling to the floor on my knees, vomiting into the toilet in my jogging bra and maternity underwear, ice stuck in the treads of my sneakers.

April 25th is my birthday. I'm thirty-two. As the best present I can imagine, Greg arranges for the boys to spend the evening with my parents. He's somewhere on the road between my parents' house and Colonial Tymes restaurant to pick up our take-out when the phone rings.

"Dr. Robb here. The results of your exam are questionable. Come on in and we'll do a biopsy."

"A what?"

"The PAP showed evidence of dysplasia on your cervix—"

There are dirty dishes in the sink. My wig is on the table. It's been four days since I've had a shower. Or looked in a mirror. I forgot I had a PAP smear. A murky memory comes to the surface of an extra-long Q-Tip, a speculum and a gallon of milk souring on the passenger seat because I'd forgotten in what order to do things. "What is dysp—"

"Pre-cancerous cells."

I sit down. I consider lying down.

"Are you telling me I have cervical cancer?"

"Not yet."

Just yesterday I drove past a new billboard on the highway: *cervical cancer: the silent killer.* Good thing I don't have that, I thought to myself.

"It's simple," Dr. Robb says like everything is breezy. "I take a cervical tissue sample and that's it. In and out. I'll have the results in a couple days."

When Greg comes home, I tell him. "Can you believe this shit?" I say.

"No," he says.

And then I start to laugh. I laugh because my shrimp tastes like metal because The Red Devil makes everything taste like metal. I laugh because I don't know why I'm trying to eat when I have a mouth full of canker sores. I laugh all the way upstairs to the shower where I sit on the floor of the tub, naked, cold water raining down because I used up all the hot water on a washing machine load of towels. I laugh because there are no dry towels.

The next day, Greg drives me to Dr. Robb's. The babies are at home with my mother and a team of aunts. One of them drives Trevor to preschool. I made lunch before dawn for the baby holders and leave it in the fridge. I tell Greg to stay in the waiting room when the nurse calls me in.

"So, are you having sex yet?" Dr. Robb says, sweeping into the room. Dr. Robb has missed his calling as a stand up.

"Ha. Ha."

"Well, you know what they say, if you don't use it, you lose it."

"No woman in history has ever misplaced her vagina," I say. At least, I say it in my head.

"How's Greg?" Dr. Robb says, turning to an enamel tray and selecting a foot-long pair of tweezers.

"He's in the waiting room."

"What? Let's get him in here!"

Yes, let's have a party and play *Operation*. I want to be the one to remove the patient's funny bone with the electro probe.

The next thing I know there's a nurse holding my left hand and Greg is holding my right.

"Relax," says Dr. Robb.

I tense.

"You're in fashion!"

"What did he say?" I ask the nurse.

"Your Brazilian!" says Dr. Robb.

The Red Devil doesn't just take away your taste buds and the hair on your head. It takes all the hair, everywhere.

"Drop your knees."

I'm being scraped with a metal blade. A *punch*. That's what it's called. Punching out tissue from the cervix. After the first punch, I don't breathe. I score the hands of the nurse and Greg with my fingernails. The second punch comes, and I wish to hover outside my body. The tweezers come out. I bleed for days.

A week later, Dr. Robb calls. I'm holding Parker. "You have dysplasia. Pre-cancerous cells." It sounds like he's talking into a coffee can.

"Dr. Robb, is it true that chemotherapy can cause false positives with PAP smears?" The night of the tissue biopsy I'd stayed up until two in the morning searching the internet.

"Yes, it's possible."

"Then I don't understand why I had a PAP in the first place." I shift Parker to my shoulder. "Dr. Robb, I'm not coming back to your office until I'm done with chemo." *And maybe, not even then.* My own voice echoes back at me. There's nothing from the other end of the phone, proof that our connection is two coffee cans linked by string. I'm not done with him though. Even though I have a mountain of health insurance papers on the table, an over-due electric bill, and four scoops of formula left, I can't hang up.

"Why did I get cancer?"

"Dr. Robb?"

"There are too many factors to fully understand—"

"Yeah. Your best guess. Off the record."

He sighs. "Well, I would say that your body was overwhelmed. It is possible that free radicals multiplied because it was distracted forming two babies and you were acutely anemic to boot. The body can only do so many things at one time."

As a modern woman, I am supposed to do everything at one time. Glass ceiling smacker, mother martyr, sex goddess, selfless sisterdaughterfriend. A cross-species planted firmly in the ground. My arms, no matter how far they are, in the kitchen or at the hospital, are wrapped around my children. My house—its shingles and sheetrock—is the taproot. My childhood, marriage, my past life, present life, and all the possibilities and limitations of a future life depend on my ecosystem not being loose. A johnny coat tied on the inside and tied on the outside. I have never been prepared for anything I've ever done.

At my next chemotherapy, Dr. Bee asks if I want anti-depressants. I don't want anti-depressants, I want sleep. When Dr. Bee's lips move I watch his words lift out of his mouth and into individual helium balloons over his head. One balloon after another.

Survival finishing Don't want watch children high ?
  means chemo you to your graduate school

I try and fail to imagine a graduation ceremony. All I see is a line of babies crawling across a stage while I hover in the lobby on hold with Jenkins-King in Ansonia, the funeral parlor where Grandma Rose was laid out in a casket, listening to Musak waiting to make my death appointment.

When I get home from oncology, the babies are screaming in their cribs. Greg leaves for a meeting and Trevor is at pre-school. I enter my bedroom to the delicate sheers and floral valances I sewed gathering dust and dead bugs because who has time to clean. The only thing to do is smash a plastic laundry basket to smithereens and call out to Grandma Rose, who was phenomenal with all babies—her own and other peoples'—pleading with her ghost to please help. To please get her great-grandchildren to sleep.

Because I don't know what to do next, I step over the wreckage of the splintered laundry basket and climb on my bed to sob. When I stop, I realize the babies have also stopped. Chemotherapy after giving birth to twins means not bonding with your babies. It magnifies the Something Else. Breast cancer detected during pregnancy while recovering from your partner's affair turns everything upside down, mashes it up, and liquifies it. Betrayal inside the body and outside the body means vacating the body. It means taking up residency in your imagination. For a year. Sometimes longer.

There is sanctity in the unknown, in the magical. I want the named to be unnamed. Like Greg's other woman, like the names of chemotherapy drugs, the names of insurance companies, the numbers on the clock, and the days of the week—all should be re-written in disappearing ink. The fissures in my body, my marriage, the foundation of our house, allow inky water to bubble up through cracks.

The seduction of space is the flatware and the way it lies in the drawer, the hallway rug and its relationship to the floor. Lamps and their bulbs, windows and doors. All the parts of the house speak with each other and live parallel to us. I touch the silverware, gather the proper number of knives, forks, spoons: we carry them to the table and lay them out. We sit at the table as a family or as one. Just me. The angle of my head in proportion to the angle of the sun coming through the window, fusing planes of the floorboards where they connect.

Which colors best paint a scene of a woman doing everything perfectly? They aren't primary, secondary, or even tertiary. They are imaginary.

Whatever is beneath the surface is being wrung out of me. I look at myself and see chaos with a bald head. Cubic zirconia earrings that I hope will distract and bitten cuticles that don't. At the twins' christening, which they sleep through the entirety of, I want to ask the minister to put a drop of water on my forehead. To make me new. Or turn me into a fish. I don't know much, but I know one thing: I can't tread water in a fetal position.

I wake gently. No one is crying. I have that feeling Christians have on Christmas morning. Before we learn that Santa Claus is made up. I'm so happy, I can't move. Something soft lands on the roof and I want to ask the ghost from my dream *what is that noise.*

In my dream, it is spring. Not real spring, Disney spring. Dressed like Snow White, bluebirds circle my head. The birds and I clean out the closet. Tucked into the peak of the gable at the front of the house, the closet has a square window. If the gable is a witch's hat, the window is its buckle. The birds tilt open the window for air. I take Greg's clothes off hangers and toss them on the bed. The birds do the same with his baseball hats.

"Look at all that space," I hear from behind.

When I turn, there is a woman sitting on the bed, holding a cup of tea and a saucer. Steam from the tea shrouds her face. The harder I try to see her, the more she dissolves. The birds bring me the stool from the bathroom—the one Trevor uses to look in the mirror when he brushes his teeth—and place it on the floor of the closet. I lift my Snow White dress, so I don't snag the hem, and step onto the stool to see out the window.

The snow is gone. Sun shines on the trees, highlighting unfurling leaves. The grass is soft and so long the breeze moves it. Everywhere I look, a flower pops up. A tulip. A hyacinth. A violet. Daffodil.

"You have to see this!" I say, turning to my tea-drinking ghost.

"I've seen it," she says shrugging.

When I look back out the window, everything's gone—the flowers, the leaves, the sun. And so is my ghost.

I don't want to get out of bed. But wait, what is that sound on the roof?

It's raining, dingbat.

I jump out of bed and snap up the window shade. It's pouring. The rain releases like Zeus has flipped a lake upside down. Rain falls on top of snow that is covered with ice. Running into the nursery, I sweep the twins out of their cribs. They are awake, and not crying, which is so shocking I want to call everyone I know. Bringing them downstairs, I feed them in my practiced method. An hour later, the twins sleeping and Trevor eating his toast, I fly to the basement.

With the ground frozen, the rain only has one place to go. Rushing towards our house's foundation, the rain pools against it, searching for one weak, soft spot to tunnel down to join the spring, which by now is likely a raging river. Two inches of water spreads across our unfinished family room's freshly laid wood laminate floor. My bare feet make rippling waves. I watch as a jagged water mark climbs up the sheetrock like a backwards, dark lightning bolt.

Opening the door to the driveway, I grab the wide shop broom and sweep the water out and down the driveway. All day. Between baby feedings, diaper changes, and throwing up, I try to turn the tide.

THIRTY-ONE

"When are you coming back? The voice on the other end of the phone is Jill, my manager at the insurance office. I'd stopped working a few weeks before Christmas, when my twin belly barely fit behind the steering wheel and my feet only fit in slippers.

Work I think to myself *a place where people get paid*. My last paycheck bought Christmas presents. Despite being a salaried employee, I have one week paid vacation. That's the whole enchilada. We've been living on infinitesimal savings and Greg's paycheck. Before the twins were born, I made forty-two thousand dollars, a few thousand more than him. The only way to pay the bills is to juggle them like a clown with bowling pins. I pray every night for the second layer on the roof to hold. For the price of gas and heating oil to stay put and for no flat tires.

The hospital bills arrive with the rain. *Baby A and Baby B amount due: $950.00*. Per day. One invoice incorrectly charges Baby B twice. I make dozens of phone calls to the hospital billing department. Deborah says, "Disregard that notice." Cathy says, "No, that bill is accurate." When I call and ask for Deborah again,

Madeline says—or is it Madeleine or maybe Madalyn—"We'll get back to you." No one gets back to me.

Our health insurance company merges with another one, so I receive duplicate bills. Then, the hospital stops billing the insurance company altogether. Instead, they send the bills to me. I owe $34,000 and some change. *Baby A, Baby B, chemotherapy, laboratory, oncology, hematology.* The collective noun for hospital bills is *assault.*

Every morning I move the Jenga pile of bills from the table to a chair. In the afternoon, I move the bills back. Organizing, labeling. The bills and the rain come and come and come.

"How's next week?" I say to Jill.

It would be a lie to say that I don't enjoy making phone calls to daycares to inquire about availability. It would be a lie to say that I hesitate to leave my three-month olds in a baby room with ten other babies who will share runny noses and ear infections.

On the drive to drop Trevor off at pre-school, the twins screaming on either side of him, he says, "Don't worry, Mom. I got this," and inserts their pacifiers. As soon as he's out of the car and I begin the fifteen-minute drive from Sunny Side Up in North Haven to The Pumpkin Patch in Wallingford, the twins open their mouths, the pacifiers drop out, and we have the final performance, a symphony for the mad. Placing the twins in professional hands, I straighten my wig in the rear-view mirror and drive the ten minutes to my office, singing the opening lines of *Amazing Grace*, the only lines I remember, my voice on repeat, echoing in the empty van.

This frantic ritual doesn't mean I can afford to pay the medical bills. It means I engage in making tomorrow's lunches, choosing tomorrow's clothes, and checking tomorrow's weather. Preparation means something is going to happen. Preparation means I may live.

It means I can flash forward in time to a day when I won't be sinking down the kitchen wall holding a screaming, colicky infant. His mouth gaping, turning his head from the bottle's nipple. To a time when I don't throw the bottle across the room only for it to bounce unsatisfactorily off a kitchen cabinet. The same cabinet I keep spices in and from now on, whenever I open it to retrieve the salt and pepper, will be reminded of my rage. Rage at myself for being a crap mother, at a doctor for nearly killing me because he didn't listen, at myself for not demanding—from the beginning—to be heard and action taken, at the limp leap of faith that the promise of sex in a Maine hotel room someday is the only thing keeping Greg from having another affair. Rage at the tales society force-feeds so I end up being unprepared for the bare knuckles of life.

By engaging in preparation, awareness dawns. I am actually alive right now—a seemingly obvious reality that, until this moment, has felt like a five-alarm rescue mission.

The money I make working three days a week, after daycare and preschool costs, amounts to less than five hundred dollars a month. It pays installments on the van. And gas. It pays for sheetrock and sponges and silence.

THIRTY-TWO

There are some moments that occur, as I hover between worlds, that bring me to terra firma. I can be anywhere in the house—some room, some chair—and be saved. This time, I'm with Spencer. He's decked out in blue footie pajamas with snaps on the inside of the legs. The zippered ones are easier to get on, but not as cute. His eyes are closed. In the dim evening light, I watch as his cheeks fill and empty. One of his dimpled hands holds my pinkie. The other is splayed on the bottle. I lean back into the rocking easy chair, my refuge.

The chair was a nighttime picker score. Hamden has bulk pick-up. For a special couple of days every spring and fall, you put whatever is too big for the regular trash out by the street. Men driving commercial trucks will haul it away, but only if the nighttime pickers don't get there first. Last March, when Greg and I were in marriage hell, I spent two nights with Caron in free furniture heaven.

Married to Greg's boss, Caron is older than me by ten years, works in community development for the city of New Haven, has a nasty four-letter word habit and a chair addiction. We hit it off immediately. When she called me after nine o'clock at night on a Tuesday to say that she'd been doing recon on a pristine Chippendale abandoned by a mailbox on Ridge Road, I grabbed the keys to Greg's truck. Rain had threatened all day but remained dry. With the chair safely in the bed of the truck Caron said, "Tomorrow will be sunny. We could really score."

During the week, Caron wears twinsets from Talbots in jewel tones that set off her pale skin and expertly cut and prematurely white hair. During the week, I wear TJ Maxx. To prepare for night number two, I donned a black turtleneck tucked into black bell-bottom yoga pants from Old Navy with a constellation of bleach spots on the ass. Caron wore a cashmere sweater and jeans, all black, all Talbots.

We slipped around the streets of Hamden in the dark. In Spring Glen—where the young Yalie parents lived—Caron grabbed my arm. "Pull over, it's a Little Tykes sandbox turtle!" Centreville— wine crates. Mount Carmel—an upholstered armchair that rocked.

At nearly every driveway entrance flanked by lights mounted on brick pillars, I pulled over, cut the lights, and Caron jumped out, throwing stuff into the truck bed. She'd jump back in, and I'd peel out. Our strategy was to pick first, look later. We turned up the radio and sang *Goodbye Earl* with the Chicks.

I tilt back further in my armchair refuge that was someone else's refuse, resting my bare toes on the foot of our four-poster where Greg lies on his back, snoring. I place my left foot on top of my right. Spencer sucks down the remaining drops of his bottle and I point my toes. In ballet class, my feet were a trophy I didn't earn, but happily displayed. The nipple falls out of Spencer's open mouth. He sleeps. I admire my arches in the beam of the streetlight.

THIRTY-THREE

Today's forecast is eighty degrees and sunny. This news joins the other gifts: it's Friday, the snow and ice has melted, and our basement is dry. I have two chemo appointments left, but I feel strong, so I tell my mother to stay home. *I'm fine.* I say. *Normal.* Which is a lie. I definitely do not feel normal. I just want to look normal. As normal as every mother taking her children for a walk.

I park in the lot at Brooksvale, a nature preserve on the cusp of tonier Cheshire, with hiking trails, goats, horses, rabbits, and a sugar shack with maple syrup demonstrations. I unload. In minutes, the boys and I are on the park's connecting bike path like any other family. A five year old on his bike with training wheels donning a huge, if crooked, helmet; twins in a tandem stroller with dual canopies; and me, smiling at my ingenuity. I managed to tie my long wig-hair into a neat ponytail at the nape of my neck. I'm even wearing sunglasses with only two scratches. Trevor is smiling and the twins kick their little legs in the sunshine.

The paved path is more crowded than I remember. Cyclists whizz past us shouting "On your left!" Marathon moms with jogging strollers sprint like gazelles. Still, it is the closest thing to normal I have experienced in a year and a half. I beam at everyone. Including two women power walking on what I assume is their lunch break. I assume this is because they are wearing sneakers with slim trousers, sleeveless blouses—one orange, the other white—and jewelry.

They don't beam back. As we pass each other, they stare at my children. The woman in white says, "My god, did you see all her kids?"

I look at my children, like they've magically multiplied. Nope. Still three.

It's getting hot. My back is sweaty. The heat feels good. So does the sweat. At the one-mile mark, I turn us around. Another pair of power walking women stare at me. Just when I begin to think bike path women hate me for having children, an older couple scowls in my direction and then look at each other, shaking their heads. I don't know what the fuck is going on. Trevor is pedaling and humming the theme song to *Rugrats*. The twins have fallen asleep.

The looks keep coming. By the time I get to the van, I'm livid. Trevor hops in the back, and I maneuver the still sleeping twins into their seats in the middle. I collapse the stroller and toss it into the trunk next to Trevor's bike and slam the hatch closed, muttering *stuck up Cheshire people* to myself. Sliding behind the steering wheel, I yank my door closed, turn the key and blast the air conditioning. Backing up, I catch my reflection in the rear-view mirror. My wig has slipped backwards. My Mediterranean bangs, instead of brushing my eyebrows, are on the crown of my head.

After work the following Tuesday, I'm on my way to pick up the twins at the Pumpkin Patch, when I stop for a red light, scratching where the wig rubs against my ear.

I wear the wig everywhere but home. Initially, I wore the wig for me, but now I wear it for other people. There is something about a bald woman that makes people—at least, the people in my world—uncomfortable. I wear it, even if they know I am bald, like at work, to put them at ease. I wait until I get home with all the children and toss the wig on the table, the stairs, the bathroom sink—wherever. The time I flung it up the stairs to the bedrooms, my mother, coming out of the bathroom, screamed. She thought it was a hamster, even though I don't have a hamster.

I've felt restricted all day. Leaning forward, I turn on the radio. I lean forward again and turn it up. I lower my window. Then I lower the passenger window. I push the button on my door that opens the van's far-back triangular windows like little wings. Finally, I peel off the wig and toss it on the passenger seat. "Yes!" I say to no one. In a minivan, everyone is invisible.

Someone screams.

An older couple is in the car next to me. The man's mouth is hanging open. The woman covers her mouth with her hand. The light turns green, and I lay on the gas.

In the remaining bald weeks of my life, red lights become the highlight of each day.

I run until it isn't fast enough. Until the end of May. Until I have just one chemotherapy left and fantasize that I will be returned to normal when it's over. I remember that I have a bicycle. It's a cheap chain-store bicycle, half of a matching pair. Greg and I bought them as part of our marriage repair and rode them once. For my last white blood cell draw, an appointment that takes a total of twenty minutes, I organize freedom. My mother has the twins at her house. Greg will pick up Trevor from pre-school. I grand jeté out of the hospital at four. By four-thirty, I'm on my bike. Radio velcroed to my arm. Earbuds firmly inserted. No wig. No helmet.

I coast downhill, past the graveyard, towards Sleeping Giant, gliding onto the Farmington Canal Trail. Pumping. On the trail, there is no one in a white coat gesturing to their diplomas, no tiptoeing husband, no children and no bills. There is only my battle-scarred arms exposed to the sun coming through the leaves. Light. Dark. Light. Dark. Freeze-frame photography—snap, snap, snap. The wheels of my bike are combustion fans. I stand and pump the pedals as hard as I can, for no reason, just because it is possible, like I am five years old again.

I don't see other people running, walking, cycling on the path. I see Diana Lane, the neighborhood where I learned to ride. My father rolls the push lawn mower out of the garage. The weather is perfect for mowing, for moving, for learning how to ride a bike. Straddling the seat, I clutch the handlebars. I've never looked so steadily at my knuckles before. They look like mountains. The pedals on my bike are metal with orange reflectors. My father starts the lawnmower engine and I start mine. My left foot on a pedal, my right foot on the curb, pedaling and hopping until I balance. Until I'm doing it. There is nothing better—not rocket pops from the ice-cream man, not cannonballs into Grandma Eva's pool. I ride up and down our dead-end street all day. When my mother tucks me in—Eskimo kiss—I ask if I will have to learn all over again tomorrow. *Once you learn, you never forget.*

At the end of the trail in Cheshire, I turn without stopping. Now, I'm in Virginia, riding my father's bike, a second-hand ten-speed red Schwinn with white lever shifters on the handlebar stem. I rip out our driveway, up Cedar Lane to the Old Dominion bike path, escaping high school, my parents, and the boy who said *I love you* to Van Halen playing on his car radio, when I said I would only have sex with someone I loved.

Heading west, I pedal past the decommissioned caboose on the Vienna town green—past suburbia. Watch: no. Sunglasses: yes. My long hair in a ponytail and five dollars in my sock for a cheeseburger and Diet Coke at McDonalds in Ashburn. I ride fifteen miles into horse country, shifting gears with my thumbs, *on your left* and *thanks y'all* in my sweet southern accent. I wave at oncoming cyclists, joggers, mothers with strollers. I say *good morning*. This is the southern way. My ponytail swings in the breeze.

I ride the road of a girl, a teenager, and a woman. The past and present rush together fusing. I recall the sensation of using my body instinctively, abstract negative and positive space become tangible, smudgeable with my thumbs. The tightness in my chest that I didn't realize was there, releases. There is only euphoria. There is only sensation. The removal of awareness of myself in relation to anyone else. Deep below, the me that had been submerged propels up out of the water, breeching like a whale I once saw off Cape Cod. I'd been shocked that a creature with so much weight could touch the sun.

I live in the shadow of a mountain whose legend is anger. Like Hobbomock, stomping his foot on the Connecticut River, I stomp my feet on the pedals. Anger is hot and cold, and haven't I been assigned roles? Devil and angel wrestling, rippling out of me as waves. My anger is tired, flat. It contrasts with the landscape of my childhood—full of pinnacles—everywhere a point was being made: a church spire, a factory tower, a castle on the head of a mountain.

I didn't think I could survive living in this new land of betrayal. The danger of anger lies in the power of its unleashing. What lies under a mountain?

Whatever it is, it's crushed.

I laugh, exiting the path, cycling toward home. Every streetlight I ride under turns on. Chemotherapy might save my life, but it can't make me feel alive.

THIRTY–FOUR

Elizabeth and I are meeting in person for the first time. We've dressed up for our lunch date at Jacob Marley's, a pub that I definitely don't need to wear my wig for, but I do. Elizabeth wears a Hermès scarf. Before I can suggest sitting outside, Elizabeth informs the hostess that *we will have a private table inside* like we are famous. We are led to a lopsided table for four in the back where sunlight slides into the room through dark wood blinds.

Elizabeth is exactly as I remember her from my glimpse in the hospital hallway months ago. She is petite with a patrician nose and full lips. Her brown eyes are full of questions. It's a look I recognize.

Once her second treatment was delayed, she enlisted the receptionist in oncology to function as my personal librarian. I'd show up for an appointment and a book would appear from under the counter. *Elizabeth left this for you.* Somehow, Elizabeth knew that I wanted to read books about surviving disasters like *Into Thin Air*, a memoir of the 1996 Mount Everest tragedy by Jon Krakauer. Or, more likely, she liked true-life survival and assumed I would. I was too grateful to care. I didn't buy books, I borrowed them from the library, so I couldn't return the favor.

Sometimes, we spoke on the phone. *How are you doing, Elizabeth* I'd ask, as if I wasn't a patient too. She asked me questions I couldn't possibly answer like *why did we get cancer* and *what if the treatment doesn't work—what would we do then* as if I wasn't a flesh and blood woman without a clue but Pythia, the Oracle of Delphi.

My replies were too banal to be encouraging. *Stuff just happens* and *we'll figure it out.* But she kept calling and now we're sitting across from each other. I order fried chicken on a Caesar salad, which comes with a fat slab of garlic bread, extra dressing and a Diet Coke. Elizabeth orders a side garden salad and water. I'm wearing jeans I haven't worn since before I was pregnant with the twins and shouldn't have. To zip them up I had to fold my stomach like my mother used to do with a soft slice of bread before dipping it into her tomato soup.

Elizabeth's inquisition begins, preluding the meal, in the form of a medical questionnaire.

Describe in detail how you told your children about your diagnosis:
I haven't. They're too little.

How many anti-nausea pills do you take?
I can't take them; they make me throw up.

How often do you call Dr. Bee between appointments?
I don't call him.

Ever?
Never.

List all the healthy food are you eating:
Chips: chocolate and potato.

What supplements do you take?
What?

Naturopathic, homeopathic—like vitamins
I don't.

Do you eat organic meat or just organic produce?
It's easier to say *just produce* than say *if I bought even one organic apple I couldn't afford baby formula.*

You ride your bike. How do you have energy?
I have no idea.

By now, the food has arrived and I begin shoveling fried chicken into my mouth and consider eating Elizabeth's salad as well. I want to talk to her like I would my mother or my cousin Alison. I want to say that I'm afraid of being a woman who does what she pleases, which would prompt Greg to leave for good. How I want to take the twins off soy formula and roll the dice with whole milk because Isomil costs a bloody fortune. How, until recently, I felt like I was drowning in a hole. That I can't fly, but riding a bike is as close as I can get. How instead of ingesting nutritional supplements, I drive my van through town in the dark, with my headlights off, spying into the windows of normal families. How I like to imagine that the onramp to the highway is a launch pad to outer space.

When my plate is wiped clean, I excuse myself to go to the ladies' room. When I return, Elizabeth meets me at the door. She's paid the bill. She hugs me and says she'll call me with the details of joining her on Nantucket for a weekend. I get in my van. She gets in her Mercedes. We wave. I know I'll never hear from Elizabeth again. Maybe I am an oracle after all.

THIRTY-FIVE

I'm on the way to the hospital for, I hope, the last time—ever. Since the second chemotherapy, I've driven myself. This is the ritual: dress up, grab the small bottle of Diet Coke I placed in our freezer for twenty-five minutes—not twenty, not thirty, twenty-five—the precise amount of time necessary to achieve a perfect alchemy of soda and ice, hop into the empty van, eject Raffi's *Singable Songs for the Very Young* and slide in *American Woman*.

It's July fifth. Since Independence Day landed on a Wednesday this year, many people, including Greg, have the week off, so morning traffic is light. Speeding onto the connector, away from Sleeping Giant, I pick up I-91 south to New Haven while thumping my hands on the wheel, swigging soda, and singing at the top of my lungs with The Guess Who.

I jog into oncology. This is my antidote to sit among dying strangers: full body vibration. I focus on my knees bouncing instead of the needle in my arm, because if I am not successfully stuck on the first try, I immediately begin to cry. Not only are my veins small, but now they are scarred from repeated piercings and like to escape needles by rolling.

For the first four infusions, I had Adriamycin and Cytoxan, a liquid chemical combo that is neon red, like a jacked-up stop light. Kathleen pushed the cocktail into the line in the crook of my left arm with a syringe. It went in cold. Like the first time, I continue to dress in a black blazer and slacks for this. As if I am going to work. Or a funeral.

For the last three infusions, I have Taxol, which is what I am receiving today, a liquid chemical that is colorless.

In the infusion room, it looks like a child's birthday party. There is a cake with yellow sugar roses and red balloons that bob across the acoustic tile ceiling. An elderly gentleman wearing a round volunteer button asks me if I would like a slice of cake. *No, thank you,* I say, *I'm not staying,* which is ridiculous, and he knows it is ridiculous, but me gives me a smile and pats my shoulder. The red balloons seem badly planned. Shouldn't they be in a color other than the poison hanging from infusion poles? I imagine how a balloon committee meeting would go.

How about yellow?

Yellow will bring out the sickly undertone of their skin.

Orange then!

Orange is for happy people. Do you see happy people in oncology?

Purple?

You fool, purple is the color of a bruise.

Balloons are for children. They are for uncles to rub on your head as if it is a plasma ball full of noble gases and a high-voltage electrode, so your hair magically shoots outward like dandelion fluff. They are for stealing into the bathroom with your cousins taking turns inhaling helium to sound like Alvin and the Chipmunks.

I sit down in a reclining infusion chair. Patients come and go. I finish my soda. My knees stop bouncing. As the seconds turn into minutes, the bubble I am in in dissolves. I notice the chilly temperature of the room and catch a whiff of the foaming liquid soap dispensed in the bathroom down the hall. Neither encourages. Both are antiseptic. My limbs stiffen. I shift because my left foot has fallen asleep. I would get up and pace if the sleepiness wasn't working its way up my leg. I push myself back from the edge of the chair and recline. Maybe there is no more treatment. Maybe I miscounted. My eyes are closing when I feel someone touching the plastic name band on my wrist. It isn't Kathleen, my reliable red-haired infusion nurse. It's someone else. This nurse places her caddy on the metal tray table next to me.

"Where's Kathleen?" I say as she pulls on purple latex gloves. My body clenches because my veins are steel with one miniature hidden door that only Kathleen can find. Instead of answering, this strange nurse turns over my left arm. Pulls her supplies from the caddy, including a red rubber strap. This is the moment that Kathleen knows I look away. This is the moment that Kathleen begins asking me if the babies are sitting up yet, or crawling, or sleeping through the night while she uses her x-ray vision on my left arm.

It always has to be the left arm, a doctor told me, which doctor I can't remember. The right side of my body can no longer be trusted. *Never let them draw blood from your right arm, not even blood pressure.* A doctor said. Which one? I walk them backward in my mind oncologist, internist, surgeon, obstetrician, because this nurse is not asking me anything, she's prodding my veins with her index finger. I can't look away.

"Just relax," she says, as if it is possible.

The needle is orange—the wrong color. All my blood vessels contract.

"Kathleen uses the purple butterfly."

She says nothing. I brace myself for the prick. I would visualize the needle going in if I wasn't staring at it. I watch the needle go in and go out and go in again. I can't breathe. All the blood that should be in my arm is in my head. Tears are coming.

"Did anyone talk with you about getting a port?" she asks.

"STOP," I say—with force behind it.

She stands up. My arm looks like a pincushion.

"Why don't you have a port?"

A port is a surgically implanted catheter. If I had one, chemo would be like self-service gas. Open the gas cap and insert the nozzle. I'd seen them on patients. Elizabeth has one. Hers is a little disk with a hole near her collarbone. When Dr. Bee suggested it, I refused immediately. A port looked like something I would never be without. A hole I could never escape.

"Where's Kathleen?" I wipe my cheek with the back of my right hand.

"Kathleen is visiting her daughter. This would be easier with a port," she says, like *I told you so*, even though I've never clapped eyes on her before. If anyone had told me that chemo shaming is a thing, I would have said they were insane.

"For you, not me," I say, cradling my arm, closing my eyes. "I would like someone else please."

I feel her staring at me, but I can win the stubborn Olympics. Usually, I take the gold. She gathers her caddy. I'm on the podium, waving to the cheering crowd.

A moment later I feel something warm. I open my eyes. There is a towel on the length of my outstretched left arm. The young nurse who is gingerly covering my legs with a blanket has sharp blue eyes and raven hair. She looks nothing like Kathleen, more like Zooey Deschanel, but her manner is so similar she could be Kathleen's twin. Let's increase your circulation, she says.

"Let's bring that blood of yours up to the surface and we'll try again."

There can be no attempting, only succeeding. This is the day I've circled on the calendar. Today is the bullseye. I have a list: final treatment, pick up babies, pick up Trevor, make dinner, make a life. I am here but I am also fast-forwarding the tape. I've already closed the door on today. But to get there, I have to open the door. Not a lot. Just a pinprick sized amount.

I recline in the chair and let the warm towel do its job. I must have fallen asleep. The towel is gone, and my new nurse is next to me. She assesses my arm and—quick—the needle is in. I watched her do it and I never saw the needle. She must be amazing at card tricks. As the poison flows in, I think about all the glorious things I won't miss. No more valet looking pained because I prefer to park my own car, no more hairlessness, helplessness or pity. I sleep deeper than I have ever slept in a chair. I sleep deeper than I have in more than a year.

I drive home alone. The van is even more empty than usual. Greg sold his truck once we found out twins were coming. We discovered that without the two bench seats, the van can do double duty. This morning before I left for the hospital, Greg got up early to ferry sheetrock from Home Depot. An empty baby bottle rolls from one side of the van to the other. When I exit the highway, a policeman has traffic stopped by the funeral home. A long line of cars with their headlights on trail behind a hearse.

Our first winter in Virginia, it snowed more than anyone had seen in decades. No one drove, there were few plows. The whole county shut down. One early morning, I sat at the kitchen table listening to the school closing announcement on the radio when the phone rang. I woke up my father. "It's Uncle Nick."

Uncle Nick wasn't really my uncle, but my father's best friend from high school. It was he who convinced my parents that Virginia was better than Connecticut. He lived nearby in Arlington.

"Get your coat," my father told me, "Nick needs us to run an errand."

The year before we moved south, my parents, sister, and I stayed at Uncle Nick's house for a long weekend. Uncle Nick and his wife Alys lived on a cul-de-sac in a large brick house with a kidney shaped in-ground pool with a hot tub on one end. The morning we were leaving for home, I saw Uncle Nick in his foyer on my way to the bathroom. Everything was black: his pinstriped suit, his tie fastened with a gold clip, his hair—slicked back and shining—and his Lincoln Continental. I assumed he worked in a bank.

I helped my dad sweep the snow off his baby: a 1975 Oldsmobile Cutlass Supreme, a black coupe with a red pinstripe. I needed two hands to open the door. Sliding the window down a crack, I tuned the radio to DC 101. With a planned future in interior design, I was looking forward to visiting Uncle Nick's office, which would be in a tall contemporary building with an indoor garden, a waterfall, and skylights, like at the mall.

My father pulled into an alley between two brick buildings. One of them had a black awning. "Stay here," he said. A couple minutes later a garage door opened, and my father drove out a yellow and brown Chevy Suburban. "Hop in," he said.

"Where are we going?"

"Uncle Nick's regular drivers can't drive in the snow, so he called me."

I squinted at my father. "Called you for what?"

"To pick up a body at the hospital."

I could be at home watching MTV, pretending to be Pat Benatar.

"Gross. So, Uncle Nick works in a funeral home," I said, shaking my head, my illusion shattered.

"Uncle Nick doesn't work in the funeral home. He owns it."

I couldn't imagine listening to Led Zeppelin in a Suburban hearse with a plow on the front and a dead body in the trunk and I said so.

"Not 'trunk,'" my father corrected. "'the back.'"

For the next two winters I was my father's co-pilot of cadavers and the coffee thermos. I was fine on the drive to the hospital, fine when my father backed into a parking spot next to a door that resembled a loading dock. I was mostly fine when he disappeared and reappeared walking backward holding a black shrouded figure on a gurney, assisted by an orderly and slid it behind me.

"How did they die?" I always asked.

"I don't know, they didn't say," he'd deadpan.

I was less than fine when we arrived at Uncle Nick's funeral home. My father would rush in to get one of the assistants, leaving me alone. Just me and a dead person in a plastic bag. My father said not to think of them as people. "They're gone," he said. *Where*, I wondered.

"Didn't it bother you," I asked him years later, when he said that he only took me on the runs that were from the hospital morgue to the funeral home. He went on runs to the crematorium by himself.

"What—did the dead people bother me? Nah. They were pretty quiet."

Then he laughed and said that the forensic doctor at Fairfax Hospital always called him *chum*. He'd watched the forensic team remove, weigh, and make diagnostic slides of internal organs. Afterwards, they placed the internal organs in a Ziploc bag and inserted the bag into the dead person's chest cavity.

The morning after my final chemotherapy, I am the bionic woman. I dust every piece of furniture, vacuum the fireplace, and wash every base molding. The babies watch from their doorway bouncers, silent, like jumping marionettes. While they nap, I toss accumulating junk in the trash, bake cookies, and scour bathroom tile. After the babies wake up, I feed them mashed bananas while simultaneously folding clothes. For my final performance, I strap the babies into the double stroller, and we take off down the hill to our happy place: the Pepperidge Farm outlet.

I buy as many loaves of bread and bags of Goldfish crackers that can fit in the stroller's basket. I buy them each a stuffed Goldfish which they gum as I jog uphill, my arms completely extended, barreling towards the finish line. The twins shriek with laughter, abandon their goldfish, and grab their toes. That night, I have a hard time falling asleep.

In the morning, I sit at the table with a piece of paper and a pen. Greg washes dishes. I'm writing a grocery list. I can't wait to shop with a regular cart instead of using the basket of the stroller for deli meat and its canopy to hold eggs. Greg talks as I write my list. So far, all I have written is *List*. He is talking about something that happened at work. Normal talking. The kind of talking partners do with each other when there is no crisis. Companionable chatter that requires no response. I turn my head and look at him. He's laughing at a joke he must have made because I haven't said a word. I want to say something. What do I want to say?

"Hey, babe?" He says, turning off the faucet.

I can't speak.

"Christine, come on—you're going to bed." His arm is around my waist and we're leaving the table. I grab my list.

"I'm going to the store," I say.

"Your head fell on the table—you aren't going anywhere."

When I was four years old I jumped on everything. I jumped as I imagined ballerinas did when they were at home. From sofa to chair to ottoman to hallway. A spine of somersaults down the hall to my bedroom where I roamed the perimeter on the tops of things: bureau to desk to the windowsill, my fingers clenching the top of the window trim. Finally, I would fall backwards onto my bed. My yellow and white afghan, knitted by Grandma Rose, smelled like Ivory detergent.

"I'm not taking naps anymore," I announced to my mother. "And I'm going to live forever."

As soon as I rejected naps, my mother made a phone call. If there was a circus in town, she might have dropped me off. Ballet was the only option. I vibrated with energy; it was my constant companion. For years I thought my shadow was evidence.

Twenty-five years later, I lie on my bed unable to move. Greg pulls down the shades and turns the air conditioner in the window next to me to the off position. The room immediately fills with summer humidity. I'm shivering. He layers me with blankets, the afghan on top. I lie beneath it all, arms straight down my sides like an effigy, pinned between consciousness and something deeper than sleep.

I hallucinate red Delicious and Granny Smith apples gleaming in an orgasmic produce pyramid. A deli counter technician dispenses Land-O-Lakes American cheese in perfect nearly see-through slices. In the magazine aisle, each beautiful woman on the cover of *Vogue, Cosmopolitan,* and *Mademoiselle*, sports peach fuzz hair like mine. I walk among this bounty, drinking it in. At the register, I donate to every charity the clerk asks. I smile at everyone and skip out into the sun.

I snap awake. According to the clock, it's ten AM. According to the note on my nightstand, Greg and our boys have gone to his mother's. I unearth myself and stumble to the bathroom to vomit. What I do next is not sleep. It is a possession. I am cold, I am hot, I want the ceiling fan off, then I want it on high. I want the windows open and the air conditioner on. I want to strip off all my clothes and peel off my toenail polish. I do none of these things. After five trips to the bathroom, I take the phone to bed. I don't have the strength to use it. It lies in my hand as I sleep.

When I wake up again, I call oncology. I've made four more trips to the bathroom. Because it is Saturday, the answering service says a doctor will respond. More sleep. Another hour. I call again. Another message. Sometime in the afternoon, the phone chirps.

"What seems to be the problem?" a deep male voice says from the dark side of the moon.

What seems to be the problem? *I'm drowning in my bed.* I force myself to sit upright. I cut to the chase. "I had my last chemo two days ago. I have a fever and I can't stop throwing up. I need to come to the hospital."

"Did you have a high yesterday?"

I think about never having tried marijuana in my life and wish I had.

"Did you have a burst of energy?" He tries again.

"Yes."

"You have a build-up of steroids in your bloodstream. There is nothing to do. It has to work its way out of your system."

I'm not bionic after all.

"I'm home alone," I say.

"Call someone," he says.

185

I hang up thinking *that's what I just did* and fall back onto the pillow.

Someone is coming up my stairs. Someone is touching my forehead. Someone is telling me *sip this water*. Someone holds a cup to my lips. Someone hovers in the doorway.

On the movie screen that is the inside of my eyelids, a red-hot air balloon is in the sky, laughing people in the basket. The hot air balloon drifts down and lands in our front yard. The laughing people aren't regular people having a good time, they are clowns. It's Halloween and the clowns are here. I watch from my bedroom window as children run up and down the street with glowsticks in their plastic jack-o-lanterns. I am the ghost in the window, which is why I am not downstairs, in my witch costume, handing out bite-sized Almond Joys and Take 5s.

The three clowns aren't kids. They are grown men. Their fake bulbous red noses keep falling off. They keep hiking up their too-big pants. They trip on their shoes. Each clown holds a slack pillowcase. The pillowcases drag on the street. The clowns look up at me in the window. *Time to bob for apples*, they say. I flip them a double bird. The cancer clowns turn their backs and moon me. Their asses aren't skin, but fabric in a pattern of crazy circles and manic polka dots.

I jerk awake. I am sitting up. Someone is walking up the stairs. "Welcome back," says my mother.

It's almost nine PM. I dangle my legs off the bed. I feel my forehead. Damp, but normal. I feel something like hunger. I stand up and look at the bed. There is a body-sized wet spot. My mother helps me bundle up the sheets and my clothes. I take a shower and use shampoo for the first time in six months. I use it everywhere, like soap. Downstairs, my mother has made me instant rice with lots of butter and salt. It tastes like manna.

"Did Greg call you and ask you to come over?" I say when she sits at the table with me. She folds a paper napkin into a triangle and slides it next to my bowl.

"No. You did. At first I thought the line was dead. Then I heard whispering. I couldn't figure out what you were saying. I shrieked your name—you scared me to death."

I called my own mother and don't remember it.

"What did I say?"

"I realized you weren't talking. You were whimpering, like a wounded animal. I hung up the phone and jumped in the car."

THIRTY-SIX

When I was nineteen and indulging in weekly seven-minute sessions at a tanning salon, my mother began cutting articles from magazines and leaving them on my bed. She attached them with metal paper clips. *Tanning Beds Kill, Toxic Shock Syndrome Murders* like a tan was the gateway drug to wearing a tampon for more than eight hours. I gave up the tanning salon, but tampons couldn't be avoided forever.

I was pulling an afternoon shift at the art store when my period came as I rang out a customer at the register. Opening my purse in the bathroom revealed no pads. I opened the sink cabinet. There was a box of tampons. The directions were missing but I navigated the contraption and went back to work.

Mary, the assistant manager, was a chain-smoking brunette with ballerina legs that she disregarded. She smoked at the loading dock with the door open, trading off-color jokes with the tattooed delivery men. When the manager hired me, Mary rolled her eyes. While advising a customer on clay, I compared the qualities of his two options.

"This one stays soft," I said pointing at a blue box. "This one gets hard," I said pointing at an identical blue box.

Mary nearly picked me up by my ears. When selling clay to men, she said with her teeth clenched, I should say this one is *malleable* and this one *hardens*.

Mary eyed me from the framing counter. "Why are you walking like that?"

I was shuffling in an aisle, straightening products.

"Are you alright?" She said. Hostile, but in a strange way, comforting.

"I've never used a tampon before." Maybe being a virgin had something to do with it. "It hurts."

"It's not supposed to hurt. You aren't supposed to feel it at all." Mary put down the frame she held and sat quickly on the counter.

"Tell me what you did. Don't leave out a single step. Tell me *exactly*."

I looked around and stepped closer to make sure no one could overhear. I relayed each step concluding, "I inserted the cardboard applicator and I pushed the cardboard up to release the cotton."

"And," Mary said, nodding, opening her palms to me.

"That's it."

"And you removed the cardboard and threw it out."

"No. It's still in there."

Mary doubled over laughing before she could help herself. She stopped and said, "Go try it again."

No one had shown me these things. I didn't have five older sisters like Mary. I had a mother who insisted I not shave above the knee with her Lady Sunbeam electric razor and stocked the top drawer of my bureau with slips and camisoles. Mary was cool and modern. I was raised to be a Victorian.

Thirteen years later, when my period unexpectedly arrives, I am not working in an art store. I am not walking through my house knowing it is coming because my breasts are sore and the vein in my right leg pulses. I am not taking Midol for a headache and also sprouting a pimple that I finger while paying the bills. When my period comes, it is five months after chemotherapy. I am in church, and I am praying.

It's a week until Christmas. We are about to sing a hymn. A Congregational hymn. *While Shepherds Watch Their Flocks by Night.* The church is packed. Greg sits squeezed on one side of me, Trevor on the other. Greg and I each hold a baby and a hymnal. Dr. Robb said that chemotherapy would likely put me into menopause, but I am not praying for my period. I am praying for patience.

Help me God, Universe, Grandma Rose. Let patience beam through the church's circa 1700s windows and hit me on the head. Penetrate the outer layer of false confidence and get to the root. So, when Spencer steals Parker's toy or Trevor can't locate his backpack before the school bus or the electrical switches burn out again for no reason we can find, I will be calm in a biblical way.

I don't have patience. I barely have hair. In Congregational churches, communion is brought to the congregation, where we sit. We are served. *Take this bread* is real bread cut into cubes. *Drink this wine.* Petite glasses, thick as eyewash cups brimming with real cabernet sauvignon passed down the pews on a stacked silver tray.

Once a month I rededicate myself. I am willing to put myself through the ten trips from the house to the van, bringing everything a five-year-old, two eleven-month-olds, and a pair of exhausted parents need to go to church for sixty minutes plus twenty more so Trevor can enjoy his reward: a bounty of all you can eat donut holes in the hall afterward. I do this for the five minutes I am capable of paying attention, swallow my bread whole and throw back the wine before I float away on lit candles, the weekly flower arrangement, and a sermon that has zero bearing on my life.

I stand to sing. Everyone stands to sing. *While Shepherds Watch Their Flocks by Night*, is a hymn I have sung all my life and a blood flood has never happened. Until now. A gush is momentarily held in by my black tights. A trickle snakes down my leg.

I have never walked out on a service. I haven't walked out on biased sermons, mediocrity, or hypocrisy. Even though I wanted to. I shoot Greg a scared look, hand him Spencer, walking only from the knees down, hoping my black skirt and tights are blood camouflage. The church is old, and the front doors are large and creak like they are rigged for broadcast.

In the bathroom of the church hall next door, I pull everything down and sit on the toilet. A fake floral frond sticks me in the back of the neck. My underwear is black so I can't see any blood but when I press my fingers to the lining they are slick. My fingers are red. There's a river of blood down my inner thigh all the way to my calf. I flush the toilet and with new toilet water, dip wadded toilet paper, applying it to my tights. I don't want attention. I'm not having great results. A trail of toilet paper bits attach to my tights like burrs. Using the rest of the toilet paper roll, I make myself a fat pad and put it on my underwear.

When we arrive home, I take the baby-sized toboggan out of the garage and place it in the snow. I sit Parker in the back and Spencer in the front. Trevor stands where a reindeer would, holding the toboggan's rope handle with both hands. He holds it delicately, as if rope could break. I drape the strap of my old Minolta around my neck and snap the picture.

THIRTY–SEVEN

It's January. The twins have just turned one and I am back in Dr. Bee's office for my first post-treatment check-up. Getting dressed this morning, I began putting on my regular chemotherapy armor, that black blazer, those black pants. Catching my naked reflection in the mirror, I stopped. Ignoring the scar across my breast and the stretch marks across my belly, I saw only the hair. Pubic hair. I finally had some. I cried.

Besides slow hair growth, there are other side effects that are slow to leave, including skin hypersensitivity. I am convinced that I can feel dust land. The metallic taste in my mouth prohibits me from enjoying chocolate, which should be, at the very least, a misdemeanor. The hair on my head is about three inches long. After an alarming fist-tight inch of curls, my hair, along with the rest of me, has relaxed a bit. My hair waves when I walk. I am excited to see Dr. Bee, exited to move out of sickness into glowing health where a giant box of Godiva with hazelnuts with no cellophane and an open lid awaits.

Well-worn jeans languish on the chair next to the exam table with a soft fitted pullover flung over them. Greg, my mother, and my father all offered to drive me, but I want to wrap the year up alone. I hug the johnny coat around me instead of tying it, pacing in my socks while I read a procedure chart for disposing syringes that is taped to the wall. My eyes land on a manilla folder on the counter next to the little sink. My name is on the tab. The intake nurse had placed it there instead of the pocket on the outside of the door. I want to open it. My next thought is *you aren't allowed.* Two years ago, or even six months ago, I would have felt bad for even thinking about opening the folder. But I'm not the same person. I open it.

On top is a letter from Dr. Robb. It outlines the dysplasia procedure and is full of medical terminology I don't understand. But I don't need to. When I returned to Dr. Robb's last month, the pre-cancerous cells had magically disappeared. I keep flipping, more letters from Dr. Robb and copies of responses from Dr. Bee. Then, the last page—a lab report. Halfway down the page I read *pathology received breast tissue and one monochorionic fused twin placenta—unremarkable.*

In the few months between learning I was carrying twins and giving birth, I read a lot of books about twins. I tried to memorize important facts, but it was mostly the weird stuff I retained. Like, in Twinsburg, Ohio there is an annual event called Twins Day Festival. And fraternal twins can be conceived at separate times by different fathers. And if identical twin girls are impregnated by identical twin boys, the children wouldn't be cousins but genetic siblings. The only important fact I retained is that a monochorionic fused twin placenta is what identical twins have in utero.

The door opens.

"Hello, young lady, what lovely hair you have."

I am hot all over. "Dr. Bee, you knew my babies are identical, but you didn't tell me?"

My personal Richard Gere walks close to me in his tassel loafers, taking the file from my outstretched hand. Whatever misgivings I once had about standing up for myself disappear—forever.

I've been saving to afford the expensive genetic test to find out whether Spencer and Parker are identical or fraternal. Looking alike isn't iron-clad. I lie awake at night worrying that one day one of them will need a kidney or a blood transfusion, but would die because I hadn't found out.

"I don't know why no one gave you this good . . ." he hesitates. I nod.

". . . news. I can only offer that the babies were born healthy, so all the effort turned to you. This isn't an excuse. Everyone forgot."

The trick for natural childbirth comes to me, the trick I never had to use. I breathe deeply and focus on a fixed object in the room—Dr. Bee's perfectly shaped bushy eyebrows.

"May I please have a copy of the pathology report?" I say, pausing between each word.

Dr. Bee knows he's dodged a bullet. "Of course!" He skips out of the room, returns with a copy, performs my breast exam, and says, "See you in six months."

I peel the minivan out of the oncology parking lot like Trevor's favorite NASCAR driver Mark Martin. Even Mark Martin would congratulate my choice of a base model Plymouth Grand Caravan over a souped-up Ford Thunderbird. I had places to go and people to bring with me.

THIRTY-EIGHT

I am in a room full of women in a three-story office building in an industrial park in central Connecticut. We are in the American Cancer Society suite for peer counselor training. We sit in a large circle and one by one, we listen to each other's stories. There is so much pain, when it is my turn, I don't relay that. I relay the plain facts. The leader instructs us to take turns counseling each other.

"There are protocols," she says, ticking them off on her fingers. "You must not give medical advice. You must not cry during a session. You must be composed and appropriate."

I can do that I think to myself *one thousand percent.* I take notes. Peer counselors can speak with patients on the phone or go to a neutral meeting place. We cannot have patients in our own homes. On rare instances, we can visit a patient in their home.

It seems to take an absurd about of time before I am assigned the only kind of patients I want—patients with young children. *I know they are out there* I say to Greg. *I can't be the only one.* Finally, the American Cancer Society calls me. I have a patient. Let's call her Fern.

I dial Fern up. Waiting for phone lines to connect, peer counselor protocol takes over. I should write down all her medications
and side-effects and after fifteen minutes of life-affirming chit-chat,
ask her if she would like me to check in on her in a few weeks to
make sure she doesn't want to fling herself out a window. Which
is how I translate the *wellness outlook* category on the intake form.

Fern answers the phone. I say who I am. Fern says, "Can I
see you?"

"Of course!" I say. I haven't even gotten to the second question
on the form.

The night before I visit Fern, I pull out my protocol binder. The
directions for home visits are clear. Be timely. Limit conversation
to twenty minutes. I may accept water, tea, or coffee. I shouldn't
accept food. I must write notes on the intake form while conversing.
At the end of twenty minutes, go home. At home, pour a goblet of
whisky and mail the intake form to the American Cancer Society.
Await further patient referrals.

My mother comes over in the morning. It's Friday, I don't work
on Fridays. Fern's house is in Wallingford, just down the street from
my insurance office. I have déjà vu when I park on Fern's street.
It's the same street my cousin Alison lived with her sister and her
mother—my godmother—when her father left. It was a tenement
house full of divorced women and feral children.

My past is present, and I have the strange sensation that it is not
my past and not my present, but other people's. I am only a witness
and exist to play some part that I haven't been prepared for. I remove
the key from the van's ignition. I feel completely inappropriate in
navy slacks, heels, white fitted T-shirt and blazer. The protocol binder
is in my giant faux-leather bag. Walking up to Fern's pretty house
with hanging plants and blooming rose bushes, I see myself in the
refection of her glass door. I'm an updated real estate agent from the
1970s in a gold Century 21 jacket and a power coiffure.

Fern opens the door, and the protocol leaves me like a puff of hot air from an oven. She hugs me. She's adorable. Petite and blonde with dimples, she wears a baseball hat and clothes so small, they must have been purchased in the pre-teen department.

When she asks if I want cake I say "Absolutely," because who in their right mind would ever refuse cake? While I shovel cake into my mouth she asks that I tell her about myself. I don't even think twice. I tell her about the flood. I tell her I almost drowned.

My bag and blazer catch my eye—they're hanging together on a hook by her front door. My binder is in my bag. I'm supposed to be writing stuff down. *Fuck.*

Without warning, Fern begins to cry. She runs out of the room. I don't know what they do at the American Cancer Society, but I follow Fern to her kitchen. She stands by the sink crying into tissues she pulls from a plywood box in the shape of a little house. The tissues come out of the chimney.

"I had a mastectomy," Fern says. "Did you?"

I am embarrassed. I only had a lumpectomy.

"Can I see?" she says.

A butcher block island is between us. Screw the protocol. I walk around the island toward her extending the neck of my T-shirt so she can see my scar. In the strange circle of discomfort, there is ease. Fern takes her shirt clean off. I see the red slash where her breast used to be. I see the look in her eyes. I know that look. I see it in the mirror every day.

I hug her. I hug her for a long time in her kitchen by the sink with the mobile her nine-year-old daughter made hanging in front of the window that faces the backyard where her kids play. I hug her through the oven timer going off and the dryer running. Fern looks at her watch. Her girls will be home from school soon. I've been there for almost two hours.

I hold it together until I get inside my van and pull away. Merging onto the Merritt Parkway, I drive home blind because of the unstoppable sobbing. I'm a crap volunteer. I should know better. When I was fifteen I wanted to be a Candy Striper. I thought it would be like TV. I found out Candy Stripers don't get to hand gorgeous neurosurgeons medical charts. They get to empty bedpans while trying not to get liquid shit on their cute pink and white striped rompers. I lasted one day.

My mother is waiting for me at my house. Over mugs of Earl Grey and a platter of chocolate chip muffins I tell my mother that I am resigning from the American Cancer Society. Visiting Fern reminded me that I am still in mourning for the body I had. If I worry about how my trauma will manifest in the future, I only have to look to my parents. My mother keeps a high-powered LED battery operated lantern on the floor by their bed. My father is forever checking their basement for seeping water. My flood waters have receded, but what is that sea creature doing there in the sand?

The twins are attempting to knock each other senseless with stuffed animals. My mother pulls Parker into her lap.

"I can't imagine I will ever make one iota of difference. I can't do it again."

My mother smooths the top of Parker's hair. He's inherited her cowlicks. "I think you can. It's possible to be completely terrified of something and do it anyway," she says, like the oracle she is.

I once worked with a woman who was about to get married. She wanted to wear her mother's silk wedding dress from 1955, but when she removed it from the box, the dress was a disaster. Large stains of unknown origin covered the bodice and full skirt. She took the dress to a seamstress. The seamstress took one look at the dress and said *water put these stains in and water will take them out*. The dress was washed, aired in the sun, and restored.

THIRTY-NINE

When I was little and sitting in front of my dollhouse, holding the mother figure I called Mrs., I mimicked in minutes what it would take me years to do as an adult. The Witch House was a life-sized version of my dollhouse, not the plain plywood one my father crafted, but the one I imagined it was, a magical castle on a hill, even if it only had one bathroom.

During the three years after my flood, the house absorbed a remodeled marriage and our family of five like a new sponge. We moved through it, touching its oak banister, raising and lowering the cloth shades, cutting and smelling the lilacs. We kept our hard angles soft, the fireplace from growing cold, and the animal inside me sleeping, tranquil as Long Island Sound.

Now that Trevor is eight and Spencer and Parker are three, the house is too small. The children grow, but the house does not. There is no thought of moving, only improving. My attachment is permanent. Together, the house and I are a mountain, something that cannot be moved. I try to make the house fit us. But like Barbies I squeezed under my dollhouse ceiling, as a family, we are outsized. My sister works for an architect with an apprentice. The apprentice comes over. He walks into every room taking pictures with an old camera. He stands in our backyard with a tape measure spanning the distance from the back door to the garage.

He designs options that I pay for with our tax return. Remove the kitchen and living room windows that face the backyard and turn them into doors, he says. Push out the back and make an open kitchen with master bed and connecting bath above. I spread the floorplan on its large white curling sheet of paper on the table and leave it there, like a precious newly discovered artifact on display in a museum. The problem is the shape of the addition: half an octagon. It has to be this way, says the apprentice. There are setback laws and ground pipes to navigate. It becomes obvious that you can't enlarge a mountain. But I don't want to say it. The house will hear me and who knows what will happen.

Greg and I whisper the truth to each other over pizza in the living room.

"Before we can list if for sale, we have to tackle the basement," he says.

He phones his youngest sister whose husband has a pool business. Help arrives in the form of a hammer drill, an electric chisel, and Portland cement. Greg and his brother-in-law work for hours in clouds of old cement dust, chiseling the cracks in the floor where water came in. When the dust clears, they pour new cement into the holes. Greg paints the walls and floors with Dry-Lok as extra insurance. The men stand in the finished basement, clapping hands on each other's backs and toasting their water taming with hard cider.

I assumed a woman would fall in love with my house, but it is a man. He once owned a chain of houseware boutiques. I remember admiring the glassware, silver, and pillows. They were simple and they were expensive.

"The house is for his son," our agent says. "He plays hockey for Quinnipiac University."

I imagine fraternity parties with beer on the floor and no one scrubbing the basket-weave tile in the bathroom the way it should be done—on hands and knees.

"The buyer won't let anything happen. He loves it and thinks you have great style."

Maybe I am making a mistake. Greg and I are only the third owners in the house's history. The first woman became a widow, the second woman moved to the Cape, Greg and I broke the curse. The house helped raise fourteen children. Fourteen children and one bathroom. I think of the two women and me together. A trifecta of house protectors. Now a hockey player with sweaty socks was going to live in our house.

At the closing, I sit, tucked like a child in a too-large banker's chair in a New Haven attorney's office. The new owners pay cash. We sign. They sign. I cry. The buyer's wife says, *aren't you sweet* when I give them the useless blueprints of the impossible addition and the skeleton key. Hiding in my purse is one cut glass doorknob.

When I was little and playing with my dollhouse, I never saw illness, or infidelity, or babies who constantly cried. I only saw that I could make whatever I needed. But you cannot make someone fall back in love with you—no matter what kind of house you live in. Falling in love again takes time and a willingness to make room for it.

About the flood of their childhoods, my parents both remember the Bailey bridges the Army Corps of Engineers erected, replacing those swept away by the swollen current. These temporary bridges, invented during war, were simple to put together, and strong enough to carry a tank.

As adults, my parents instinctively sought out the safety of tall things—houses on hills, the view from the cab of a tractor trailer. Mountains.

Greg is my tall thing.

To accept that forgiveness is possible, I built a bridge, even if temporary, over my raging emotions until they receded. When your defenses are down and your life, or what you love, is threatened, you grab whatever is nearby. I have my voice. I am still using it.

The legacy of trauma, if you survive, is resilience.

EPILOGUE

There is a cycle to water. There is a tide. There is the washing of babies, of laundry, and of wounds. There is a point of critical mass when the rains come too fast, riverbanks overrun, husbands make mistakes, doctors misdiagnose—basements flood. Houses have lives of their own.

A few years after selling The Witch House, I hear from Margie that the current inhabitants have twins. I drive by the house. The contents of my basement—their basement—are spread all over the driveway. There is water everywhere.

ACKNOWLEDGEMENTS

No one forgives you like family and no one attends your spoken word performances or poetry readings like family. To my biggest supporter, my husband Greg and our talented, empathetic, and brilliant children: Trevor, Spencer, and Parker—you are my four greatest loves. To my mother Carol, father Alan, and sister Heather, for their steadfast encouragement, even if they think I am crackers.

To Paul Toussaint, for asking me to read some of my early (and fairly crappy) essays at his amazingly inventive and sorely missed arts space the Empty Spaces Project. To Michael Klein, whose encouragement gave me guts. To Melissa Wyse, devoted reader, sage advice-giver, valiant letter-writer, and dear friend. To Nichole Danis, for bike rides, bitch hikes, and for not giving up on me.

To Christine Pakkala, for her memoir workshop. But most of all, for following me into the bathroom and whispering from her stall to mine *you are a writer*. The best thing that could ever happen sitting on a toilet.

ABOUT THE AUTHOR

Before earning an MFA from Goddard College, Christine was a seamstress for the interior design industry.

Essays, flash nonfiction, and poems have appeared in *The Culture We Deserve, Longreads, The New Guard*, and *The Connecticut Literary Anthology,* among others. She has taught writing at Westport Writers' Workshop, Manhattanville College, and through free community outreach in a hospital, libraries, and once in an antique building where she had to stoke a fire.

Christine lives in Pomfret, Connecticut with her husband Greg and their dog Virginia Woof. She is working on her next book.